Oxford English for Cambridge Primary

2

Sarah Snashall

Oxford University Press

OXFORD
UNIVERSITY PRESS

Great Clarendon Street, Oxford, OX2 6DP, United Kingdom

Oxford University Press is a department of the University of Oxford. It furthers the University's objective of excellence in research, scholarship, and education by publishing worldwide. Oxford is a registered trade mark of Oxford University Press in the UK and in certain other countries

© Oxford University Press 2016

The moral rights of the authors have been asserted

First published in 2016

All rights reserved. No part of this publication may be reproduced, stored in a retrieval system, or transmitted, in any form or by any means, without the prior permission in writing of Oxford University Press, or as expressly permitted by law, by licence or under terms agreed with the appropriate reprographics rights organization. Enquiries concerning reproduction outside the scope of the above should be sent to the Rights Department, Oxford University Press, at the address above.

You must not circulate this work in any other form and you must impose this same condition on any acquirer

British Library Cataloguing in Publication Data
Data available

978-0-19-836626-3

11 10 9 8 7 6

Paper used in the production of this book is a natural, recyclable product made from wood grown in sustainable forests. The manufacturing process conforms to the environmental regulations of the country of origin.

Printed in China by Golden Cup

Acknowledgements
The questions, example answers, marks awarded and/or comments that appear in this book were written by the authors. In examination, the way marks would be awarded to answers like this might be different.

The publishers would like to thank the following for permissions to use their photographs:

Cover: GK Hart/Vikki Hart / Getty Images; p24: Tibor Bognar/Alamy; PhotoBliss/Alamy; p28: gresei /Shutterstock; topseller / Shutterstock; lsantilli / Shutterstock; nella / shutterstock; robynmac / Shutterstock; Gruffi / Shutterstock; p29: svry / Shutterctock; p52a: John Birdsall/AGE Fotostock; p52b: Blue Jean Images / Alamy; p52c: Bubbles Photolibrary/Alamy; p70a: auremar/Shutterstock; p70b: Glow Asia RF/Alamy; p71: Maxime Bermond / Getty Images; p72: STR New/Reuters; p78: JONATRONIX; p82: cobalt88/Shutterstock; p83: JONATRONIX; p98(t): Peter Stroh / Alamy; p98(b): sad444 / Shutterstock; p98(b/g): Vaclav Volrab / Shutterstock; p108: iadams / Shutterstock; p114a: Ken Lucas/Getty; p114b: Sergey Uryadnikov / Shutterstock; p114c: Franco Banfi/naturepl.com; p116: Tom Soucek / Alaska Stock / Corbis; p116(b/g): Mazzzur / Shutterstock; p117(b/g): Ralph Loesche / Shutterstock; p117: WWF-Indonesia & Klaus Lang; p118: Eduard Kyslynskyy / iStock; p120: Juniors Bildarchiv GmbH/Alamy; p122(t): Anup Shah / naturepl.com; p123(b/g): OUP; p122(b): David Keith Jones/ALAMY; p123a: Dane Glasgow / Shutterstock; p123b: Andrew Bignell / Shutterstock; p123c: Pierre-Jean Durieu / Shutterstock; p124(t): al teravagimov / Shutterstock; p124(b): DOELAN Yann / Getty Images; p126-127: David Keith Jones/ALAMY; p128: Julie Langford / www.limbewildlife.org

Artwork is by: Roberta Angaramo, Ilias Arahovits, Micha Archer, Beatrice Bencivenni, George Black, Andy Catling, Katriona Chapman, Pippa Curnick, Steve Dorado, Laura Ellen Anderson, Steve Horrocks, Cathy Ionescu, Tamara Joubert, Mike Love, Alan Marks, Gustavo Mazali, Luciana Navarro Powell, Dusan Pavlic, Claudia Ranucci, Yannick Robert, Kimberly Scott, Jon Stuart, Kristina Swarner, Stephen Waterhouse

The author and publisher are grateful for permission to reprint the following copyright material:

John Agard: 'I'd like to squeeze', copyright © John Agard 1996 from *All the Colours of the Earth* (Frances Lincoln Books, 2004), and 'Flying Fish', copyright © John Agard 2002, from *Under the Moon and Over the Sea* (Walker Books, 2009), reprinted by permission of the author c/o Caroline Sheldon Literary Agency Ltd.

Clare Bevan: 'Name That Dragon' from *Fairy Tale Poems by Clare Bevan* (Macmillan Children's Books, 2009), copyright © Clare Bevan 2009, reprinted by permission of the author.

Valerie Bloom: 'Water Everywhere' from *Let Me Touch the Sky: Selected Poems for Children* (Macmillans Children's Books, 2000), copyright © Valerie Bloom 2000, reprinted by permission of the author c/o Eddison Pearson Ltd.

Paul Cookson: 'My Football' from *Pants on Fire* (Macmillan Children's Books, 2005), copyright © Paul Cookson 2005, reprinted by permission of the author.

Bashabi Fraser: 'My Mum's Sari' from *Walking With My Iguana* (Wayland Hachette, 2009), copyright © Bashabi Fraser 2009, reprinted by permission of the author.

Monica Gunning: 'Classes under the Trees' from *Not a Copper Penny in Me House* (Macmillan Children's Books, 1994), copyright © Monica Gunning 1994, reprinted by permission of the author.

John Hegley: 'Tree Poem' from *My Dog is a Carrot: a book of poems* (Walker Books, 2007), copyright © John Hegley 2002, reprinted by permission of United Agents (www.unitedagents.,co.uk) on behalf of John Hegley.

Wes Magee: 'On the Playground' from *Stroke the Cat: a Collection of Poems* (Quarto Books, 2004), copyright © Wes Magee 2004, reprinted by permission of the author.

Eithne Massey: *The Dreaming Tree* (O'Brien, 2009), copyright © Eithne Massey 2009, reprinted by permission of The O'Brien Press Ltd, Dublin.

Pratima Mitchell: *Raju's Ride* illustrated by Stephen Waterhouse (Oxford Reading Tree, OUP, 2005), text copyright © Pratima Mitchell 2005, illustrations copyright © Stephen Waterhouse 2005, reprinted by permission of the author and Oxford University Press for the illustrator.

Michael Morpurgo: extracts from *The Dancing Bear* (HarperCollins, 1994), copyright © Michael Morpurgo 1994, reprinted by permission of HarperCollins Publishers Ltd.

Grace Nichols: 'Granny, Granny, Please Comb my Hair' and 'Crab Dance' from *Come Into My Tropical Garden* (A & C Black, 1988), copyright © Grace Nichols 1988, reprinted by permission of Curtis Brown Group Ltd, London, on behalf of the author.

Michael Rosen: 'Over My Toes' from *Bananas in My Ears: A Collection of Nonsense Stories, Poems, Riddles and Rhymes by Michael Rosen* (Candlewick Press, 2012), copyright © Michael Rosen 2011, reprinted by permission of Walker Books Ltd, London SE11 5HJ.

Pauline Stewart: 'Goodbye Granny' from *Poems Around the World 1* collected by Brian Moses and David Orme (Collins, 1999), copyright © Pauline Stewart 1999, reprinted by permission of the author.

Any third party use of this material, outside of this publication, is prohibited. Interested parties should apply to the copyright holders indicated in each case.

Although we have made every effort to trace and contact all copyright holders before publication this has not been possible in all cases. If notified, the publisher will rectify any errors or omissions at the earliest opportunity.

Links to third party websites are provided by Oxford in good faith and for information only. Oxford disclaims any responsibility for the materials contained in any third party website referenced in this work.

Contents

A world of stories, poems and facts — 4

Unit contents — 6

1. **Fiction** New friends — 8
2. **Non-fiction** Party time! — 24
3. **Poetry** Everyday poems — 40
4. **Fiction** World stories — 52
5. **Non-fiction** How things work — 70
6. **Poetry** Caribbean trip — 86
7. **Fiction** Mountain bear adventure — 98
8. **Non-fiction** Animal world — 114
9. **Poetry** Wordplay poems — 130

Reading fiction
Raju's Ride — 142

You can find the audio for the extracts and poems in this book by going to:
www.oxfordprimary.com/oecpaudio

A world of stories, poems and facts

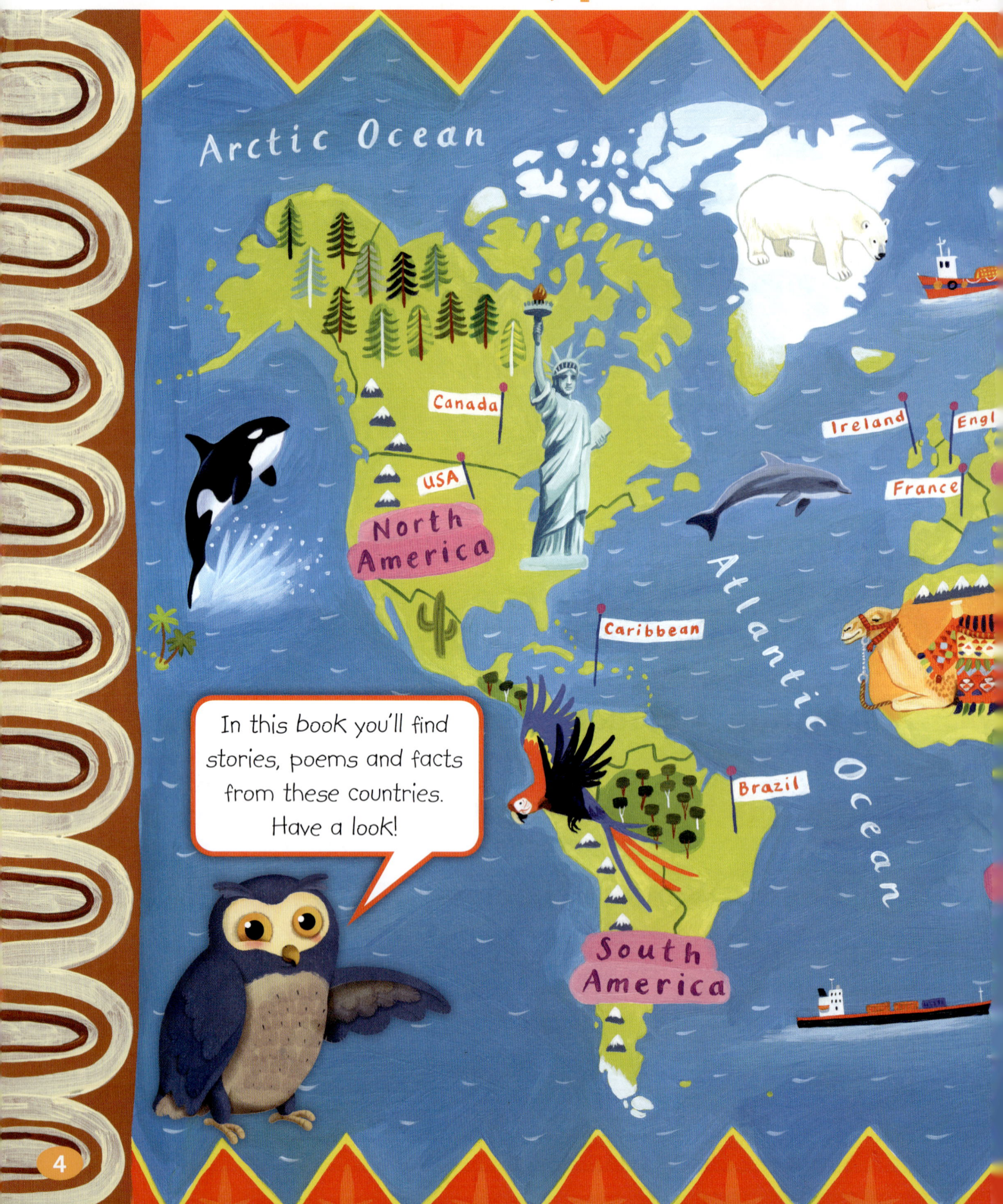

Arctic Ocean

Canada

USA

North America

Caribbean

Ireland

England

France

Atlantic Ocean

Brazil

South America

In this book you'll find stories, poems and facts from these countries. Have a look!

Russia
Asia
Northwestern China
Iraq
India
Tanzania
Java
China
Japan
Pacific Ocean
Indian Ocean
Oceania
Southern Ocean

Unit contents

Unit	Theme	Reading and comprehension	Writing
1	New friends	**Fiction** Narrative with a familiar setting *The Dreaming Tree*	Fiction Planning a story with setting, characters and structure story with beginning, middle and end
2	Party time!	**Non-fiction** Instructions *Party To Do list, Invitation, How to get to my house, How to Make a Pizza, The Great Coin Trick, Dancing Dragon Puppet*	Non-fiction Writing instructions
3	Everyday poems	**Poems** Playtime poems *On the Playground, My Football Counting Rhyme, My Mum's Sari, Goodbye Granny, Supermarket*	Poetry Writing a poem
4	World stories	**Fiction** Traditional narratives from around the world *How Bear Lost His Tail, The Golden Slipper*	Fiction Writing a traditional story
5	How things work	**Non-fiction** Explanations *Exploring Volcanoes, How to Create a 3D World*	Non-fiction Writing an explanation
6	Caribbean trip	**Poems** Poems by significant poets *I'd Like to Squeeze, Flying Fish, Classes Under the Trees, Water Everywhere, Crab Dance, Granny Granny Please Comb My Hair*	Poetry Writing a poem
7	Mountain bear adventure	**Fiction** Narrative by significant author *The Dancing Bear*	Fiction Planning a story with a sequence of events Evaluate and edit story plan
8	Animal world	**Non-fiction** Non-chronological reports *Amazing Leatherback Turtle Facts, Animals in Danger, Red Pandas in Danger, Ngorongoro Crater*	Non-fiction Writing report facts
9	Wordplay poems	**Poems** Poems with language play *Over My Toes, Tree Poem, Name That Dragon, Night-lights*	Poetry Writing a list poem

Language, grammar, spelling, vocabulary, phonics, punctuation	Speaking and listening
- Blend sounds - Connectives, *and, but, because* - Two-letter phoneme, /ar/ - Extending range of interesting words and phrases to describe	Questions – developing ideas and explaining further Recounting experiences Expressing ideas precisely
- Instructions vocabulary - Common suffix, *–ly* - Blend sounds - Language of time - Sentence punctuation: capital letters and full stops - New words in context	Questions – developing ideas and explaining further Expressing ideas precisely Including relevant details Attentive listening
- Rhyming patterns - Long vowel phonemes, /igh/ /ee/ /oa/ /ai/ /oi/ /oo/ - New words in context - Alliteration - Features of poetry genre	Questions – developing ideas and explaining further Expressing ideas precisely Trying out different ways of speaking Speak clearly about likes and dislikes in reading poetry
- Long vowel phoneme, /ou/ - Connectives, *because, do* - Verbs past tense - Language of time - Compound words - Interesting words and phrases to describe people - Significant words - Respond to question words	Questions – developing ideas and extending understanding Recounting experiences Expressing ideas precisely Extending experiences through role-play Including relevant details Vary talk to hold listener's attention Show attentive listening
- Long vowel phonemes, /ee/ /ai/ /igh/ - Verbs - Connectives, *so, because, but, when* - Interesting and significant words and phrases - Features of explanation texts - Question words and question marks	Questions – developing ideas and extending understanding Recounting experiences Expressing ideas precisely Including relevant details
- Rhyming words, sounds and rhythm - Alliteration - Spelling common word ending, *–ing* - Interesting and significant words and phrases - Features of poetry genre - Adjectives - Compound words	Expressing ideas precisely Including relevant details Listening carefully, responding and asking questions of others
- Common suffix, *–ly* - Simple adverbs - Language of time - Interesting and significant words and phrases - New words in context	Questions – developing ideas and extending understanding Expressing opinions and ideas precisely
- Features of non-chronological reports - Finding factual information from charts and diagrams - Verb tenses - Significant and technical words - Subheadings and paragraphs - Syllables - Connectives, *and, if, because, when* - Adjectives	Questions – developing ideas and extending understanding Expressing opinions and ideas precisely
- Digraph, *sl* - Rhyming words - Features of poetry genre - Adjectives - Common spellings of /igh/ phoneme	Reciting poems Expressing opinions precisely

Fiction Speaking and listening

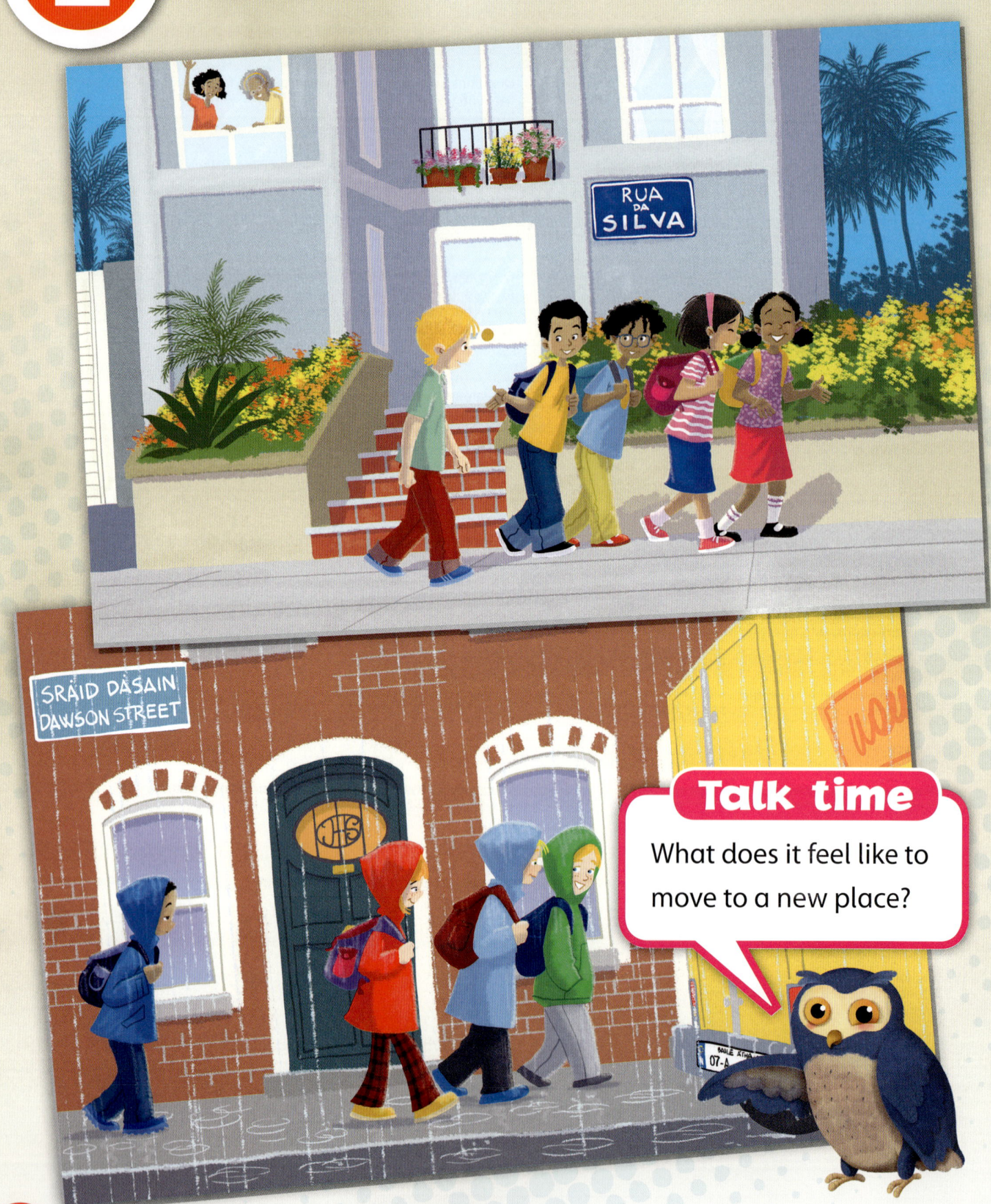

1 New friends

Talk time

What does it feel like to move to a new place?

Fiction Vocabulary

A Choose words from the box below to describe the two pictures on page 8 and write them in the correct bubble.

> sunny   wet   dry   cloudy
> dull   bright   warm   cold

Rua da Silva

Sraid Dasain/ Dawson Street

B Choose a word from the box to complete each sentence.

> homesick   fun   excited   scary
> shy   lonely   happy

1 Making new friends can be _____.

2 When you move house you can feel _____.

C Write three words of your own to describe the place where you live.

_____   _____   _____

9

Fiction Reading

The Dreaming Tree
Eithne Massey

Roberto and Amanda were on their way home from school. …

Amanda … dragged her schoolbag along the ground. She whined.

"You are going too fast," she said. "I can't keep up."

It was true. Roberto was walking as fast as he could. He wanted to get through the park quickly. He did not want to see the boys playing football. They were always there. They never asked him to come and play.

The biggest boy was called Fergus. Fergus was telling the players what team they were on. Today it was the World Cup. Fergus was the captain of the Irish team. He was always the captain. He always got the best players. The goalie, Shane, was his brother. Shane was the same age as Roberto.

Roberto thought he looked nice. He smiled at Roberto and Amanda as they went past.

When they got home their mother was very excited because their grandmother was going to telephone that afternoon.

"You can both talk to Vovó on the telephone," she said.

Roberto and Amanda had been born in Rio de Janeiro [in Brazil]. Their grandmother still lived there. Roberto missed her a lot.

Vovó came on the phone to Roberto. Even though they often spoke English at home now, Roberto and Amanda always spoke Portuguese to their grandmother. She didn't speak any English at all.

She said: "So, you have been in Ireland all summer now. How is your new school? Have you made any friends?"

"Not really," said Roberto.

"But you must," said Vovó. "Why go all across the world if you don't make friends? Would you like a friend?"

"Of course I would," said Roberto.

"Well, I have an idea," said Vovó. "You remember the story I told you?"

"Which story?" said Roberto. Vovó had told him many, many stories.

"The one about the Dreaming Tree," said Vovó.

"Tell me again," said Roberto.

"There once was a boy who found a tree in a forest. There were all sorts of different animals lying in it. …

"All of the animals were fast asleep. … None of them woke up when the boy climbed into the tree. He fell fast asleep too. He dreamed that he met a big black jaguar. It was the Jaguar King! The Jaguar King taught him many things. When the boy woke and left the tree he had become very wise. He knew how to get his heart's desire."

"What's a heart's desire?" asked Roberto.

"It is what you really, really want," said Vovó. …

"So, do I have to find a jaguar?" said Roberto. "I don't think they have them here."

"No, you have to find a tree," said Vovó.

He asked his mother if he could go out to the park to play.

"Go ahead," she said. "But be sure to be back by four o'clock. And come home if it starts to rain."

Roberto went to the park. … But he didn't go to where the boys were still playing football. Instead he thought about his grandmother's story. He found a big tree …

Roberto climbed up into the tree. He felt as if he were a bird in a nest.

The green leaves moved in the sunlight. They went backwards and forwards, backwards and forwards. The green branches swayed in the wind. Rocking him. Backwards and forwards, backwards and forwards.

He could hear water flowing and the sound of the branches moving in the wind and the voices far away. He fell fast asleep. He dreamed about all the animals his grandmother had told him about.

Roberto opened his eyes. A face was peering at him through the leaves. It was a jaguar! The jaguar was huge and black. Roberto looked into its slanted green eyes. They were the same colour as the leaves around its black face.

The jaguar opened its mouth in a huge yawn. Roberto could see its white teeth and pink tongue and dark throat. He could hardly breathe. Then he heard a strange noise. The jaguar was purring loudly. It stretched itself.

"I am Sinaa," it said. "The Jaguar King. What do you want?"

"I want a friend," said Roberto. The Jaguar King smiled.

Roberto opened his eyes. Everything was darker. The leaves were a darker green. The sky was a darker blue.

"It must have been a dream," he thought. "I must have been asleep."

Fiction Reading

But he could still hear purring. He could still see green eyes looking at him through the leaves. He could see white teeth and a pink tongue. But there was no jaguar there. Just a very large, fat, black cat.

It was curled in the branches of the tree. It was yawning, as if it had just woken up. Then it stretched itself.

Roberto could hear voices calling.

"Snowy, come here Snowy, here Snowy … good cat." It was Fergus.

"Come here, why don't you?" he called again.

Roberto peered down through the branches. Fergus and Shane were beneath the tree, looking very worried.

Shane said, "Where could she have got to?"

"She'll be all right," said Fergus.

"She might not be," said Shane. "She has been missing for ages. She could have her kittens any minute."

Roberto looked at the cat. The cat looked at Roberto.

"Come here, little cat," he whispered. The cat came over to him. She let him lift her up.

He scrambled down the tree. It was hard to keep a grip on the cat. But he made it. The two boys jumped when he appeared out of the leaves. Then they saw the cat.

"Is this your cat?" Roberto asked. But he didn't need an answer.

Shane had taken the cat in his arms. He was hugging her tightly. Roberto hoped he wouldn't squeeze the kittens out. Shane and Fergus were smiling at him. Roberto smiled back. …

The next day, Roberto walked home through the park by himself. … He went past the place where the boys were playing football.

"Hey, come over here," said Fergus.

Roberto went over.

"Do you want to be on the Irish team?" asked Fergus. …

Roberto thought for a minute. Ireland had never made it to the World Cup Final. Not once. Brazil had won the World Cup. Five times. …

"I usually play striker," Roberto said. "Is that ok?" Fergus nodded his head.

The sun was shining. Roberto pulled off his jacket. His shirt was green and yellow today. It had five gold stars on it.

Word Cloud
jaguar
slanted
striker

Fiction Comprehension

The Dreaming Tree

A Read and respond

Circle the correct answer to each of these questions.

1 Where was Roberto born?

> Rio de Janeiro   China   England

2 What does Vovó tell Roberto to find?

> a tree   his sister   a football

B Read and respond

Find clues in the story to show how Roberto feels at the beginning and the end of the story and write them in the boxes.

Beginning

Fiction Comprehension

End

C What do you think?

1 Why do you think Roberto was walking quickly at the beginning of the story?

_____

2 Why was Shane so worried about Snowy?

_____

3 How do you think Roberto felt when Fergus asked him to be in the Irish team? Give reasons for your answer.

_____

_____

Fiction Vocabulary and grammar

Word detective

A Choose one of these words to join each pair of sentences.

and   but   because

1 *He wanted to get through the park quickly. He did not want to see the boys playing football.*
He wanted to get through the park quickly _____ he did not want to see the boys playing football.

2 *They were always there. They never asked him to come and play.*
They were always there _____ they never asked him to come and play.

3 *He was always the captain. He always got the best players.*
He was always the captain _____ he always got the best players.

4 *Roberto and Amanda always spoke Portuguese to their grandmother. She didn't speak any English at all.*
Roberto and Amanda always spoke Portuguese to their grandmother _____ she didn't speak any English at all.

> Sentences start with a **capital letter** and end with a **full stop**. Words that join sentences together are called **connectives**.

Fiction Spelllling and phonics

B Find words in the story that have the letter group **ar** and the long **/ar/** vowel sound. Write the words in the correct column.

> In some words vowels have short sounds, as in 'apple'. In other words, they have long sounds, as in 'car'. Say the words aloud to check the vowel sound.

ar at the beginning of the word, e.g. **ar**t	**ar** in the middle of the word, e.g. p**ar**t	**ar** at the end of the word, e.g. f**ar**

Fiction Vocabulary

C Find three words or phrases in the story that describe the jaguar. Circle the one that you think is the most interesting.

_____

_____

_____

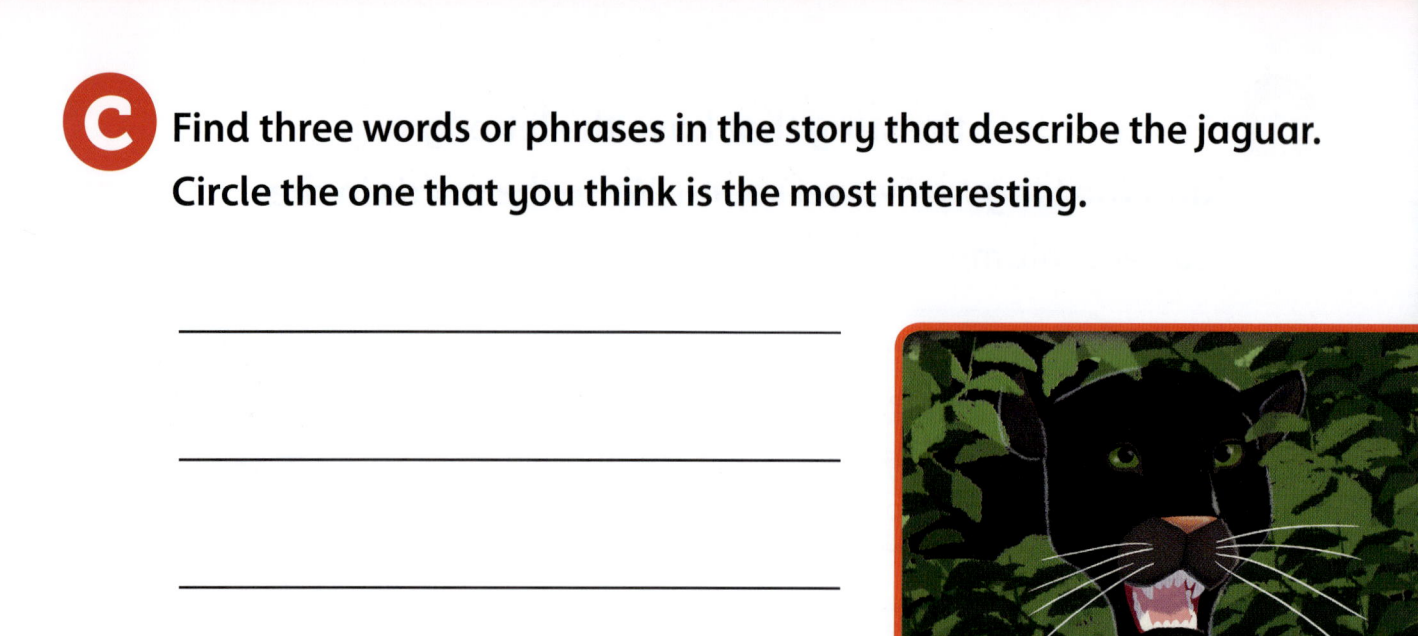

Now choose the two words you think are the most interesting from the box below. Then use them in a sentence of your own about the jaguar.

> big   enormous   scary   terrifying
> powerful   strong   nice   magnificent

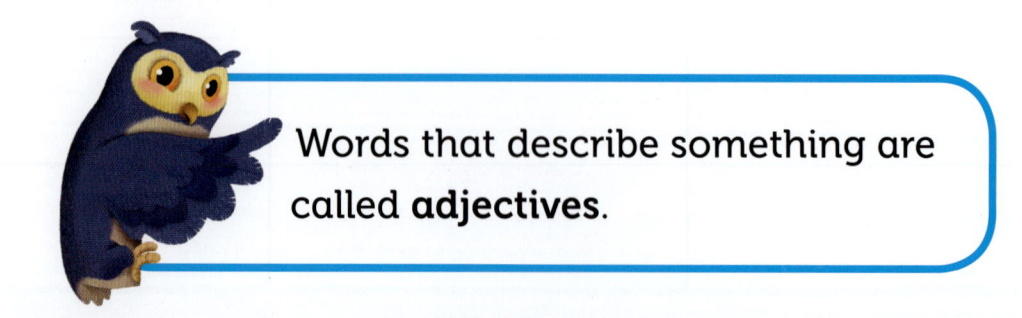

_____

_____

Words that describe something are called **adjectives**.

Fiction Writing

Get writing

Plan a story set somewhere you know well.

Part 1 Familiar setting

Choose one of these settings for your story.

Describe three things about your setting, such as the things or people you can see there.

_____

_____

_____

_____

> Don't forget to use adjectives to describe the things or the people in your setting.

Fiction Writing

Part 2 Main character

Draw your character

Write notes about what your character is like. (Are they shy, kind, funny, silly, naughty, mean, sensible or something else?)

_____

What does your character like to do? (Do they like to play sports, read, chat on the phone, draw, play computer games or something else?)

_____

What is your character's name?

_____

What is your character's heart's desire?

_____

Fiction Writing

Part 3 Story plan

Use these questions to help you to plan your story.
Write your plan on separate paper.

Beginning
Where is your character? What is he or she doing?
Do they see something?

Middle
What happens next? Does your character get lost?
Do they meet someone? Do they get given something? Do they feel frightened or excited?

End
How does your story finish?

When you have finished your plan, read it aloud to check it makes sense. Can it be improved?

Use your plan to tell your story to your partner.

Non-fiction Speaking and listening

2 Party time!

Talk time

What is your favourite celebration? Explain why.

Non-fiction Reading

Party To Do list
- Write invitations
- Make piñata
- Decorate house
- Buy party food
- Make pizzas
- Choose party games
- Practise my party trick

Word Cloud
decorate
piñata

Invitation

Please come to my party

When: 2pm, Saturday 1st February

Where: 47 Park Lane

Hope you can come!

May

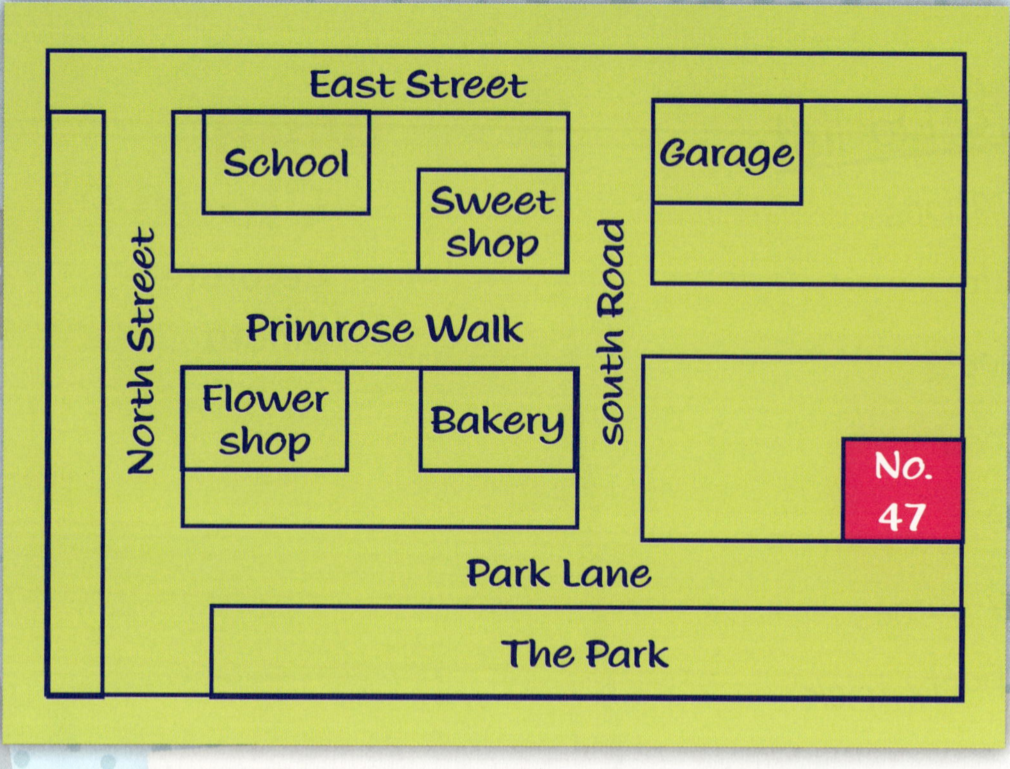
East Street
School
Sweet shop
Garage
North Street
South Road
Primrose Walk
Flower shop
Bakery
No. 47
Park Lane
The Park

How to get to my house

1 Come out of the school and turn right.

2 Take the first road on the right, which is called South Road. You will see a garage on the corner.

3 Cross over Primrose Walk and keep going straight. You will see a bakery.

4 At the end of the road you will come to Park Lane. Turn left.

5 Walk down the road for two minutes. You will see number 47 on your left. It's a yellow house.

Non-fiction Comprehension

How to get to my house

A Read and respond

Use the street map on page 26. Start at the school and follow these directions.
Turn left out of the school. Take the first turning on the left.
Carry on to the next corner. Cross over the road. Where are you?

_____

B Read and respond

Your mother wants to buy some bread on the way to the party.
Write directions for getting from the school to the bakery.

_____

_____

_____

C Read and respond

Choose a place on the map. Give your partner directions to get there from the school. Make your directions as clear as possible and use these time words: First, Next, Then.

Did your partner end up at the right place?

Non-fiction Reading

How to Make a Pizza

This recipe makes a pizza for four people.

You will need:

One pizza base

Tomato paste

400g of mozzarella cheese

2 fresh tomatoes

Fresh olives

1 red pepper

A handful of fresh basil leaves

What to do:

1) First, ask an adult to pre-heat the oven to 220° Celsius.

2) Spread the tomato paste over the pizza base.

3) Next, ask an adult to slice the cheese into thin slices. Place them on top of the tomato paste.

4) Now ask an adult to slice the tomatoes, olives and red pepper. Place them evenly across the pizza.

Non-fiction Reading

5. Tear up the fresh basil leaves and sprinkle them over the pizza.

6. Finally, ask an adult to place the pizza in the oven. Cook the pizza for 10 minutes, or until the cheese has melted and begun to turn brown.

Careful – the oven is hot. Ask an adult to help you.

7. Ask an adult to remove the pizza carefully from the oven, allow it to cool, then serve.

Eat the pizza hot or cold.

Word Cloud
mozzarella
spread
sprinkle

Non-fiction Comprehension

How to Make a Pizza

A Read and respond

1 How many grams of mozzarella cheese are needed for the pizza?

   _____

2 How many people does this recipe feed?

   _____

B Read and respond

1 What do you put on the pizza after the tomato paste?

   _____

2 How should the pizza be taken out of the oven?

   _____

Words ending in –ly often tell us how something is done.

C What do you think?

Why do you think the tomatoes, olives and red pepper need to be placed evenly on the pizza?

_____

_____

Non-fiction Vocabulary

Word detective

Instruction words are 'bossy' **verbs** that tell us what to do.

A

1 Find three instruction words or 'bossy' verbs in **How to Make a Pizza**. Write them here.

_____   _____   _____

2 Find these three features in **How to Make a Pizza**. Tick them when you have found them.

Numbered points ☐   What to do list ☐   Headings ☐

B   Add the letters –*ly* to the words below and use the new words to fill the gaps in the sentences.

thin   smooth

1 Slice the cheese _____ before putting it on the pizza.

2 Spread the tomato paste _____ over the pizza base.

Clear language makes instructions easy to understand.

31

Non-fiction Reading

Dancing Dragon Puppet

You will need:
A piece of A4 sized red card (you will need to cut this in half lengthwise)
A piece of A4 sized green shiny card
Pencil
Scissors
Glue
Sticky tape
Coloured pens and glitter for decoration
Two drinking straws (not bendy ones)

1. First, take your long piece of red card and make a small fold in one end.

2. Now turn the card over and fold it in the other direction.

3. Carry on until you have folded your card into a concertina shape.

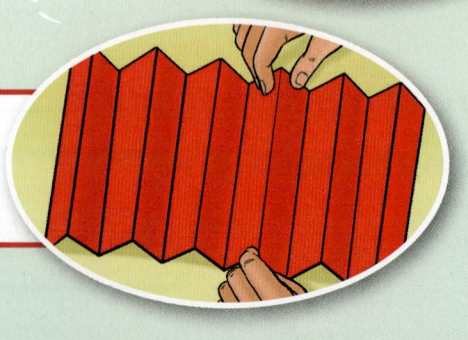

Non-fiction Reading

4 Next, draw a dragon's head and tail on the green card. Decorate them with coloured pens and glitter.

5 Cut out the dragon's head and tail.

6 Then, glue them to either end of your red concertina.

7 Glue the straws to the back of the head and tail. Add some extra sticky tape to make sure they are secure.

8 Finally, take a straw in each hand and make your dragon dance for Chinese New Year.

Word Cloud
concertina
lengthwise
shiny

Non-fiction Comprehension

Dancing Dragon Puppet

A Read and respond

Cross out the things that you do not need to make a Dancing Dragon Puppet.

> green shiny card   glue   pencil   paint   straws
> black paper   scissors   sticky tape   string

B Read and respond

1 Why do you need a pair of scissors?

   _____

2 When do you need to use the sticky tape?

   _____

3 What do you use the straws for?

   _____

C What do you think?

Why is the card in the middle of the dragon puppet folded into a concertina? What does this mean you can do with the dragon? Discuss your ideas with a partner.

Non-fiction Vocabulary and punctuation

Word detective

Time words help us follow the order of the steps.

A Find these time words in **Dancing Dragon Puppet**. Tick them when you have found them.

First ☐   Next ☐   Finally ☐

B Rewrite the following instructions in the correct order, adding time words, capital letters and full stops.

glue them to either end of your red concertina
cut out the dragon's head and tail
draw a dragon's head and tail on the green card

1 _____

2 _____

3 _____

C Find these words in **Dancing Dragon Puppet**. With a partner, talk about what you think they mean.

direction   decoration   secure

Non-fiction Writing

Get writing

Part 1 My pizza

Write instructions for making a pizza.

Don't forget to add a heading and use numbered steps and time words.

_____

_____

_____

Non-fiction Writing

Non-fiction Writing

Part 2 How to make a Chinese lantern

Rewrite the instructions listed below next to the correct picture. Add time words to help readers follow the order of the steps.

You will need

Coloured paper

Scissors

Glue

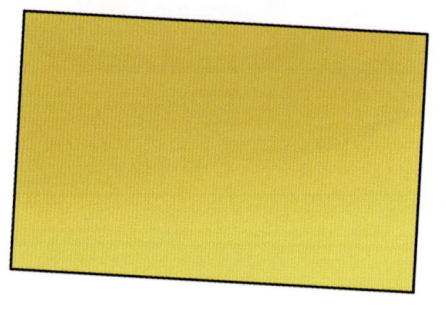

- Cut some lines along the fold end.
- Fold the paper in half.
- Stick the handle on the inside of the lantern.
- Cut a strip of paper to make a handle. Put glue on each end.
- Open out the paper. Glue the short sides together.

What to do

1 _____

_____

2 _____

_____

Non-fiction Writing

3 _____

_____

_____

4 _____

_____

_____

_____

5 _____

_____

_____

When you have finished writing your instructions read them aloud to your partner. Have you included time words? Ask your partner if your instructions are clear. Could they be improved?

Make more lanterns and hang them up!

Poetry Reading

3 Everyday poems

On the Playground

Children bumping
Children thumping
Children jumping, jumping, jumping

Children creeping
Children weeping,
Children leaping, leaping, leaping

Children crashing
Children bashing
Children dashing, dashing, dashing

Children hopping
Children flopping

(there goes the bell!)

Children... stopping.

Wes Magee

My Football Counting Rhyme

I kicked my football
Once against the wall
Twice in the bathroom
Three times in the hall

Four times in the kitchen
Five times at the door
Six at my sister
Then seven more

Eight against the gate
Nine against the slide
Ten against the greenhouse
And then I had to hide!

Paul Cookson

Word Cloud
greenhouse

Poetry Comprehension

A Read and respond

Re-read My Football Counting Rhyme. Tick the box to show whether the sentence is true or false.

	True	False
He kicked the football six times in the kitchen.	☐	☐
The football smashed the greenhouse glass.	☐	☐
He had to hide the football.	☐	☐

B Read and respond

With a partner, read **On the Playground** and **My Football Counting Rhyme** aloud. Then take it in turns to read out your favourite line and say which poem you like best and why.

C What do you think?

With a partner, read the two poems again, this time clapping along with the beat or rhythm of the words as you read. Which do you think has the strongest rhythm?

_____

_____

Poetry Vocabulary and spelling

Word detective

A compound word is made up of two smaller words joined together.

A Find the following compound words in **My Football Counting Rhyme**. Then split the words into the two words that make them.

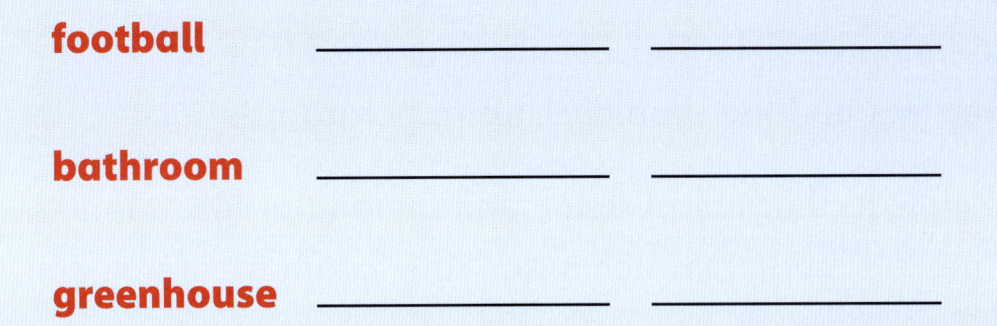

football _____ _____

bathroom _____ _____

greenhouse _____ _____

B Long vowel sounds can be spelled out by different letter groups. Underline the different ways the long vowel sound is spelt in each pair of rhyming words below. Then draw a line between the two words. The first one has been done for you.

cr<u>ee</u>ping   toys
wait   bite
sight   l<u>ea</u>ping
coat   wrote
boot   gate
noise   fruit

C Find words in **My Football Counting Rhyme** that rhyme. With your partner, talk about the rhyming pattern.

43

My Mum's Sari

I love my mother's sari on the washing line
Flapping like a giant flag, which I pretend is mine.

I love its silky softness when it's folded to a square
Which I can roll into a ball and pretend it isn't there.

I love to hold its free bit that swings over Mum's back
And wrap it round my shoulders, like a potato in a sack.

I love the pleats that fall in shape and spread out like a fan
Where my kid brother crouches and says 'catch me if you can'.

I love to wash my dirty hands at the kitchen sink
And wipe them on Mum's sari before she can even blink.

But when she takes her anchal* and ties it round her waist
I know it's time for battle and a quick escape is best!

Bashabi Fraser

*anchal is the lower edge of a sari

Word Cloud
crouches   pleats
flapping   sack

Poetry Comprehension

My Mum's Sari

A Read and respond

Write down one thing that the child loves to do with her mum's sari.

_____

B Read and respond

What does 'quick escape' mean in the last line of the poem?

_____

C What do you think?

Find an example of two words in **My Mum's Sari** that are close together and start with the same sound. Write the two words on the lines below. Then discuss with a partner why the poet chose to put these words together.

_____ _____

> Poets sometimes put words that start with the same letter or sound close together. This draws attention to the words and the sounds they make.

Goodbye Granny

Goodbye Granny
It's nearly time to fly
goodbye Granny
I am going in the sky.
I have my suitcase
and things.
You have packed
me everything
except the sunshine.
All our good times
are stored
up inside
more than enough
for any plane ride.
Goodbye Granny
things will be all right
goodbye Granny
I won't forget to write.
Goodbye Granny
bye! bye!
bye! bye!

Pauline Stewart

Poetry Comprehension

Goodbye Granny

A Read and respond

Find words that start with the same sound that sit next to each other in the poem.

_____   _____

B Read and respond

Does the boy live close to Granny? How do you know?

_____

_____

C What do you think?

Where do you think the good times are stored?

_____

_____

Poetry Reading

Supermarket

I'm
lost
among a
maze of cans
behind a pyramid
of jams, quite near
asparagus and rice,
close to the Oriental spice,
and just before sardines.
I hear my mother calling, "Joe.
Where are you, Joe? Where did you go?"
And I reply in a voice concealed among
the candied orange peel, and packs of Chocolate Dreams.

Word Cloud
asparagus   concealed
candied   sardines

Poetry Reading

"I
hear
you, Mother
dear, I'm here –
quite near the ginger ale
and beer, and lost among a
              maze
                of cans
                  behind a
              pyramid of jams
           quite near asparagus
         and rice, close to the
      Oriental spice, and just before sardines."
                      But
                      still
                my mother
             calls me, "Joe!
         Where are you, Joe?
        Where did you go?"

"Somewhere
  around asparagus
  that's in a sort of
        broken glass,
          beside a kind of messy jell
            that's near a tower of cans that fell
              and squashed the Chocolate Dreams."

Felice Holman

Poetry Comprehension, speaking and listening

Supermarket

A Read and respond

Look for the speech marks " " before and after the words that are spoken.

With a partner, read the poem aloud, taking it in turns to take on the roles of Joe and his mother. Each time Joe's mother repeats his name, make your voice louder.

B Read and respond

With your partner, work out what happens to the jam, the cans and the Chocolate Dreams at the end of the poem.

C Read and respond

Find the following types of poems in this unit and write their names. (You can use the same poem more than once.)

Can you find…?	Name of poem
A poem that rhymes	_____
A poem with a strong rhythm	_____
A poem that paints pictures in your mind	_____
A funny poem	_____

50

Poetry Writing

Get writing

Using the three-line pattern that is used in **On the Playground**, write a two verse poem about being back in the classroom after playtime. You can use some of the rhyming words below to help you.

snoring	drawing	storing
talking	walking	squawking
playing	saying	laying
throwing	sowing	blowing

_____

_____

_____

_____

_____

_____

When you have finished your poem, read it aloud to yourself. Change any lines that don't sound right.

Fiction Speaking and listening

4 World stories

Talk time

What is your favourite story? Is there someone in your family who tells you stories?

How Bear Lost His Tail

A tale from North America retold by Sarah Snashall

In the first days, when the world was new, Fox and Bear were the best of friends. Bear had the longest, fluffiest tail you could imagine. He would swish it this way and that and all the animals loved Bear and his tail. The animals spent their days playing together. The forest was warm and there was lots of food to eat.

But then the first winter came and with it came the first trouble. Snow covered everything. There was frost on the berries and ice covered the lake and Fox and Bear couldn't find anything to eat. Soon they were very hungry and very cross and so they began to argue. The animals became jealous of Bear's tail and Fox was the most jealous.

Fiction Reading

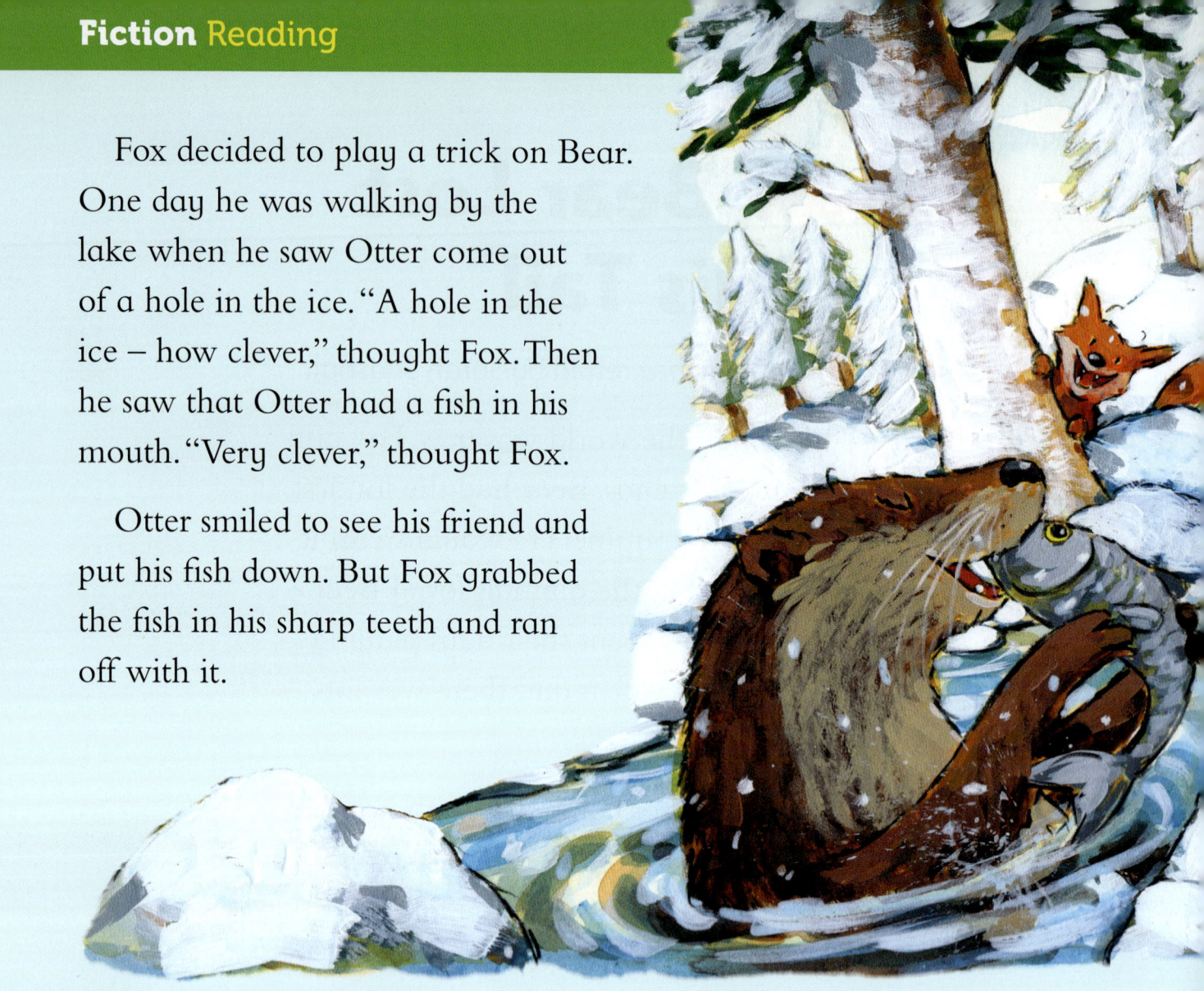

Fox decided to play a trick on Bear. One day he was walking by the lake when he saw Otter come out of a hole in the ice. "A hole in the ice – how clever," thought Fox. Then he saw that Otter had a fish in his mouth. "Very clever," thought Fox.

Otter smiled to see his friend and put his fish down. But Fox grabbed the fish in his sharp teeth and ran off with it.

Never had a fish tasted so good. He had nearly finished it when who should come along but Bear.

"Hello, Bear," said Fox. "You've just missed lunch."

"How did you catch a fish?"

"It was easy. I'll show you," said Fox, with his nicest smile. "I made a hole in the ice and put my tail in. The fish nibbled on my tail and I pulled out my tail, fish and all. Your tail is so long you'll catch even more fish than I did."

Fox made a hole in the ice and helped Bear to put his tail into the freezing water.

Fiction Reading

"Now stay there and don't move a hair. I'll hide behind this tree and tell you when your tail is covered in fish and then we'll have a feast!" said Fox. But he didn't hide behind the tree – he went back home and laughed and laughed.

Bear sat as still as he could, dreaming of the fish he was going to catch. Soon his tail started to tingle but he waited for Fox to call him. His tail tingled more and Bear imagined it covered in juicy fish. At last Bear could stand it no longer and leapt up. But, oh, his tail had frozen in the water and snapped off completely. Bear looked at his tail with horror.

"Fox!" he cried. He looked behind the tree. When he saw that Fox was not there he knew that it had been a trick. He roared with anger and ran off to find Fox. But he was nowhere to be seen.

Since that day, Bear has trusted no one. He keeps to himself, grumpy and sad.

Word Cloud

argue   nibbled
fluffiest   swish
horror   tingle
jealous

Fiction Comprehension

How Bear Lost His Tail

A Read and respond

1 When is the story set?

Now ☐   Long ago ☐   Not long ago ☐

2 Which animal did Fox see with a fish in its mouth?

_____

B Read and respond

Draw a line from each character to the word that best describes their personality.

kind   trusting   mean   silly

Fox

Bear

Fiction Comprehension, speaking and listening

C Read and respond

Use the story map to tell your version of the story to a friend. Include some words spoken by the different characters, using different voices for each character.

3 Fox grabbed the fish and ran off with it.

4 Fox lied to Bear about how he caught the fish.

5 Bear put his tail in the icy water.

7 Bear was angry and went off to find Fox.

Fiction Phonics and spelling

Word detective

A Read the following words from **How Bear Lost His Tail** and then circle those that have the long **/ou/** vowel sound.

> you   would   thought   out
> trouble   mouth   jealous

The letter group '**ou**' can be pronounced in different ways. Say the words aloud to hear the different sounds.

B The long **/ou/** vowel sound can also be spelled with the letter group **'ow'**. Find the words in the story that have the **'ow'** letter group and then circle those with the long **/ou/** vowel sound.

_____   _____   _____

_____   _____   _____

C Think of two other words that have the long **/ou/** vowel sound and then use them in two sentences of your own.

_____

_____

Fiction Grammar

Word detective

Most stories are written in the **past tense**. Verbs in the past tense often end in *-ed*. When a verb ends in *e*, we drop the *e* before adding *-ed*.

A Find the right verbs from the story to complete these sentences.

1 Snow _____ everything.

2 Fox _____ to play a trick on Bear.

B Rewrite the following sentences, changing the verbs into the past tense.

1 The animals play together in the forest.

_____

2 Fox walks by the lake.

_____

C Choose one of the following verbs and then use it in the past tense in a sentence of your own.

taste   roar   laugh   nibble

_____

Fiction Reading

The Golden Slipper

A tale from Iraq **retold by Sarah Snashall**

Once upon a time in Iraq lived a girl called Maha. When she was young, her mother died and her father, a kind fisherman, took a new wife – a stepmother for Maha. Her name was Hutun and she was jealous of Maha. From sunrise to sunset, Hutun made Maha wash, sweep, cook and mend whilst she and her daughter slept, ate and shouted.

One day, Maha was carrying a basket of fish home when she heard a frightened cry coming from the basket. "Please throw me back into the river. Let me live!" said the voice.

Maha gasped and carefully put down the basket. There amongst the fat grey fish was a little red fish, gasping for breath.

Maha gently placed the little red fish back into the river. As it swam away, the fish turned to her and said, "Thank you, kind girl. If you need help, come to the river and call me."

Weeks passed by. Maha often crept to the riverbank and told the little red fish her sorrows. The little red fish's wisdom and friendship gave her strength. One day she said, "Oh little red fish, all the ladies in the town have gone to the merchant's daughter's henna party. I so want to go but I am not beautiful enough and I have nothing to wear."

At once the little red fish dived down and returned with a bag which it threw onto the riverbank. "Your beauty is your kind heart. Here are clothes to match it."

In the bag, Maha found a green dress of the smoothest silk and a pair of golden slippers. She washed and changed and ran to the party.

As Maha entered the henna party room, all the women turned to stare at such a beautiful woman. No one knew who she really was. "I'm sure I have seen her before," Hutun whispered to her daughter.

Maha, feeling happy for once, watched the dancing, ate delicious dates and baklava and listened to the chatter. When she saw her stepmother leaving, Maha quickly thanked the hostess and dashed to get home first. In her hurry, she tripped and one of her golden slippers fell into the river. She got home just in time to change her clothes.

Fiction Reading

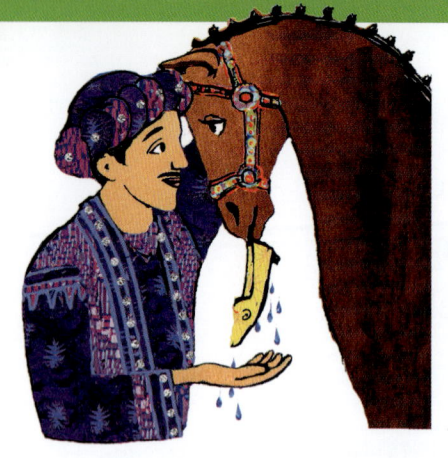

All night, the lost slipper bobbed along the river, then stopped near the royal palace. At daybreak the prince's horse nibbled at it as he took a drink. When the prince took the delicate, tiny slipper in his hands, the beauty of it filled his heart. He rushed home and begged his mother to help him find its owner.

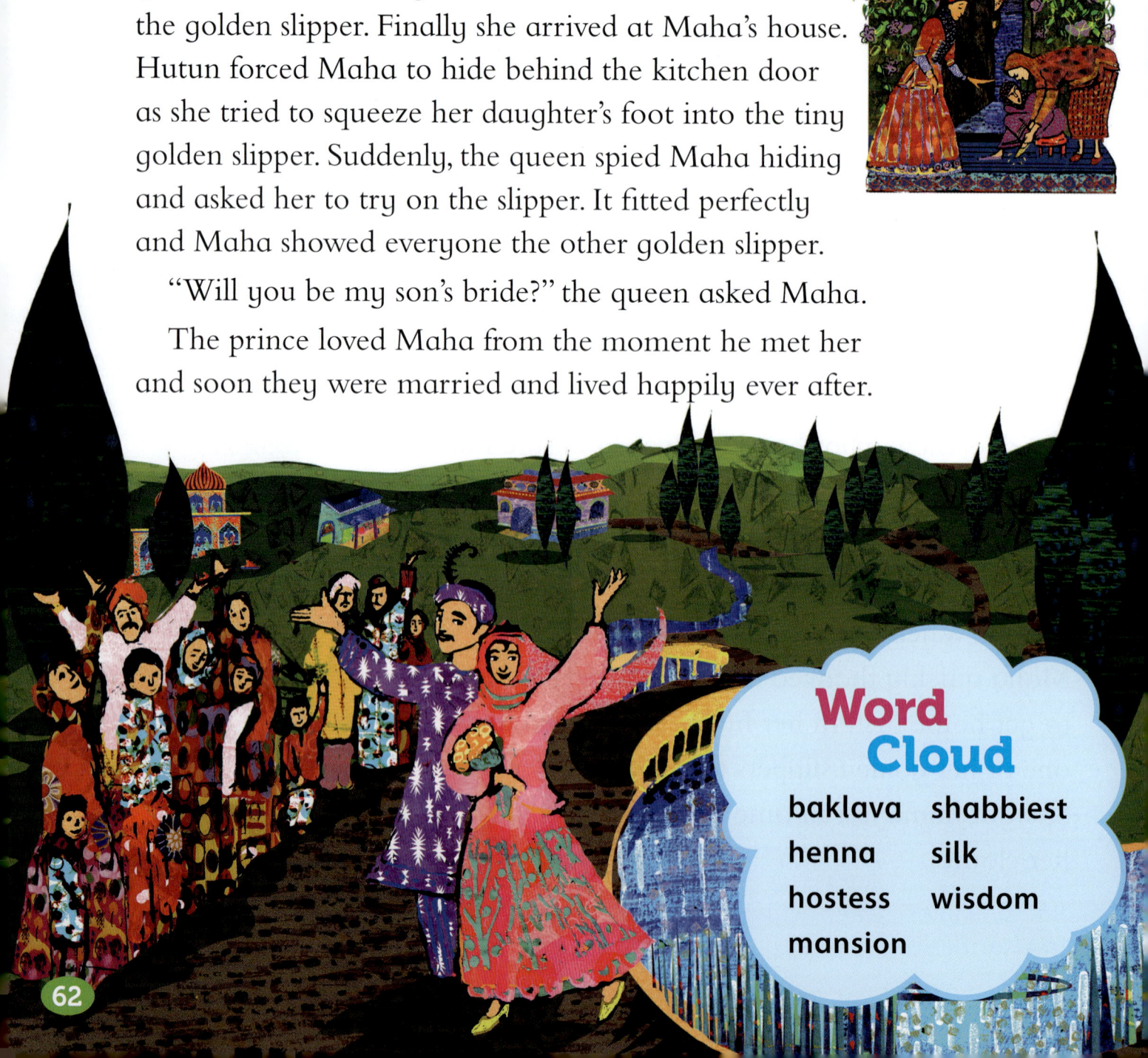

From the richest mansion to the shabbiest shack, the queen searched throughout the town for the owner of the golden slipper. Finally she arrived at Maha's house. Hutun forced Maha to hide behind the kitchen door as she tried to squeeze her daughter's foot into the tiny golden slipper. Suddenly, the queen spied Maha hiding and asked her to try on the slipper. It fitted perfectly and Maha showed everyone the other golden slipper.

"Will you be my son's bride?" the queen asked Maha.

The prince loved Maha from the moment he met her and soon they were married and lived happily ever after.

Word Cloud
baklava   shabbiest
henna   silk
hostess   wisdom
mansion

Fiction Comprehension

The Golden Slipper

A Read and respond

Find four phrases that tell you this story is set in a different time and place from your own.

_____

_____

_____

_____

B Read and respond

With a partner, pretend to be Hutun and her daughter after Maha gets married. What do they say to each other?

> Do you think Hutun and her daughter are happy for Maha?

63

Fiction Comprehension

C What do you think?

Answer these questions. Write your answers in clear sentences, remembering to use capital letters and full stops.

1 Why was the stepmother mean to Maha?

_____

2 Why did the red fish want to help Maha?

_____

3 Why do you think Hutun told Maha to hide when the queen arrived?

_____

_____

Fiction Vocabulary

Word detective

A Find these compound words in the **The Golden Slipper**. Split each word into the two smaller words that make it.

daybreak _____ _____

riverbank _____ _____

B Find four time words or phrases in **The Golden Slipper**.

> In stories, time words tell readers when something happened and help the story to move along.

_____ _____

_____ _____

C Replace the word 'and' in these sentences with a connective from the box.

> because   so

1 Maha was kind to the fish [and] _____ the fish helped her.

2 The queen went to Maha's house [and] _____ she wanted to find the owner of the slipper.

65

Fiction Vocabulary

Word detective

Find at least three of each of these types of words and phrases in **How Bear Lost His Tail** and **The Golden Slipper**.

Time words and phrases

Interesting words for 'said'

Interesting words for movement

Fiction Writing

Get writing

Write the next part to the story **How Bear Lost His Tail** in which kind Otter teaches Bear to catch fish.

Part 1

Look at this snowy scene. Imagine you are there. Use the words to help you write a description of the scene.
How would you start your story? Try to choose interesting words and phrases.

- paw prints in the snow
- frozen lake
- thick snow
- branches covered with snow

_____

_____

_____

_____

67

Fiction Writing

Part 2

What are Otter and Bear like? Write some words and phrases to describe them in the boxes. Use the pictures and story to help you.

Part 3

Plan each stage of your story. Write the words and phrases you are going to use next to each picture on page 69. Try to use interesting words and include some words that one of the characters might say. Use a separate piece of paper if you want to write more.

> Before you start writing, discuss your ideas with your partner. Can your story be improved?

Fiction Writing

Title of story: _____

_____

_____

_____

_____

_____

_____

69

Non-fiction Speaking and listening

5 How things work

Talk time
What was the last explanation you gave?

Non-Fiction Reading

Exploring Volcanoes

A volcano is a mountain with an opening at the top where hot air, ash, gases and lava come up from deep within the earth.

When a volcano is erupting, it is called an active volcano. Up to 70 volcanoes around the world erupt each year. It is dangerous to be near an active volcano, yet there are people who live very close to them.

World's most dangerous volcanoes

Name	Country	Interesting fact
Vesuvius	Italy	Erupted in 79 CE. Ash covered nearby towns, including Pompeii.
Merapi	Indonesia	Smoke comes out of this volcano at least 300 days a year.
Sakurajima	Japan	Many tourists go to see the lava flows on this mountain.
Galeras	Columbia	Nine people were killed at the top of this volcano when it erupted suddenly in 1993.

About 3 million people live near Mount Vesuvius in Naples, Italy.

Inside an active volcano, the air is hot and full of toxic gases. It is not safe for people to go in or near one. So how can people study and explore volcanoes if they can't go inside them?

71

Non-fiction Reading

Dante II

Dante II is a robot which is used to explore the inside of a volcano. People safely remain outside while they direct the robot where to go and what to do inside the volcano.

Dante II moves around and records information. This information is sent back to the control room. Inside the control room a computer uses the information to work out how hot the gases are inside the volcano. This information can help people to work out how soon the volcano may erupt. Dante II can also collect rock samples.

Scientists prepare Dante II to explore Mount Spurr in Alaska.

Non-fiction Reading

A close-up of Dante II

The **video camera** takes pictures inside the volcano.

The **winch drum** has 300 metres of cable wrapped round it.

A **long cable** allows the robot to move up and down while being tied to the rim of the volcano.

It has **eight legs** which have been built for walking and climbing over rocky ground.

Word Cloud

- CE
- control room
- erupt
- lava
- rock samples
- toxic
- winch drum

73

Non-fiction Comprehension

Exploring Volcanoes

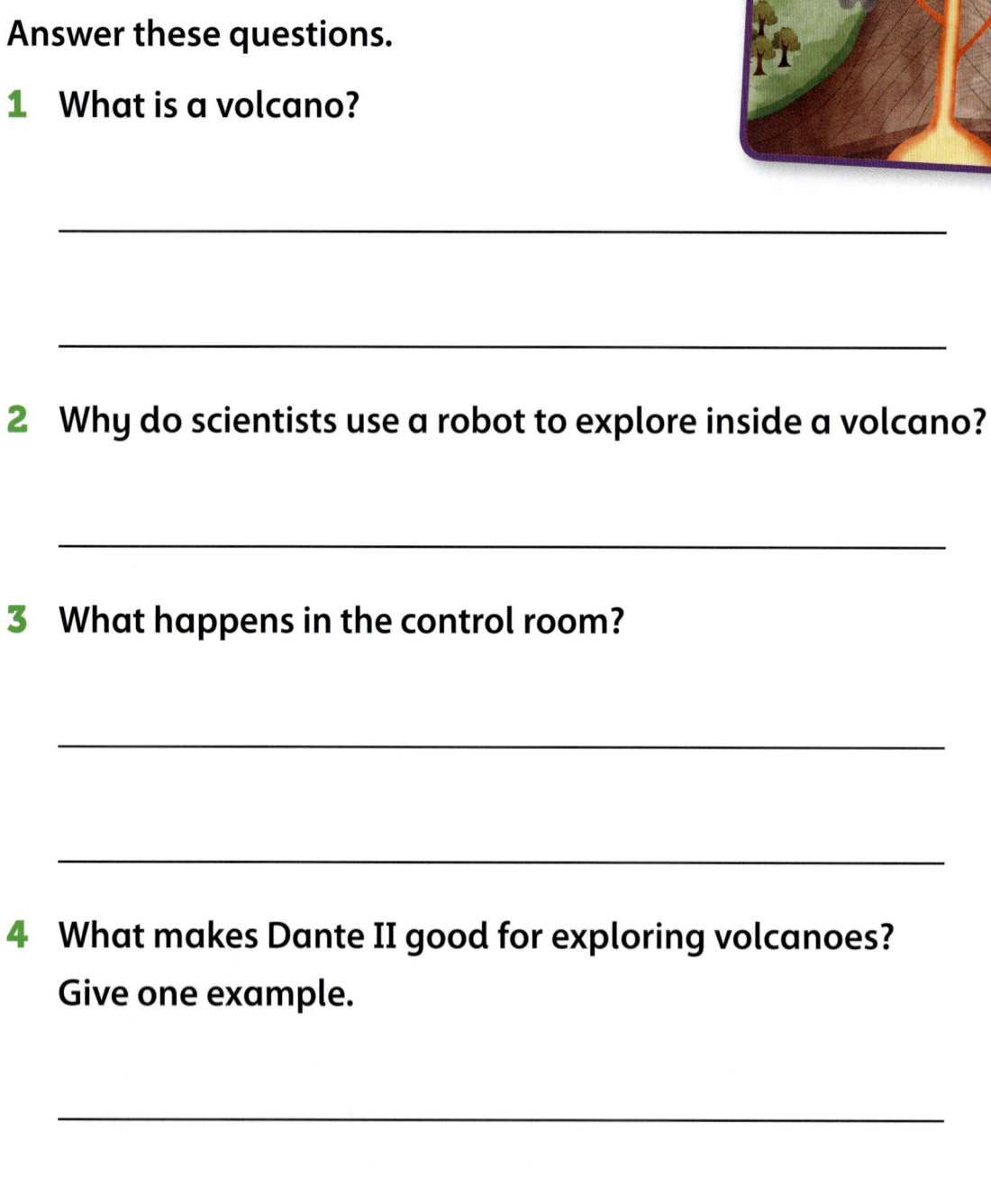

A Read and respond

Answer these questions.

1 What is a volcano?

_____

_____

2 Why do scientists use a robot to explore inside a volcano?

_____

3 What happens in the control room?

_____

_____

4 What makes Dante II good for exploring volcanoes? Give one example.

_____

_____

Non-fiction Comprehension

B Read and respond

Draw a line from the information to the section you find it in.

Information	Section
General information about volcanoes	Chart (page 71)
Dangerous volcanoes around the world	A close-up of Dante II diagram (page 73)
The parts of Dante II	Introduction (page 71)
Information about the people who live near Mount Vesuvius	Caption to photo (page 71)

C Read and respond

Re-read the section of text on Dante II on page 72. Write notes on the information in this section, including some key words and phrases from the text.

_____

_____

Non-fiction Vocabulary

Word detective

Remember, a **connective** is a word that joins two parts of a sentence together.

A Choose the best connective to replace 'and' in each sentence.

so   because   but   when

1   Active volcanoes are dangerous **[and]** _____ some people live close to them.

2   It is not safe to go inside an active volcano **[and]** _____ the air is full of toxic gases.

3   Dante II has eight legs **[and]** _____ it can climb and walk over rocky ground.

4   The robot records information **[and]** _____ it is inside the volcano.

Non-fiction Phonics, spelling and grammar

B Find two words from the text on pages 71–73 for each of these long vowel sounds and write the words in the correct volcano.

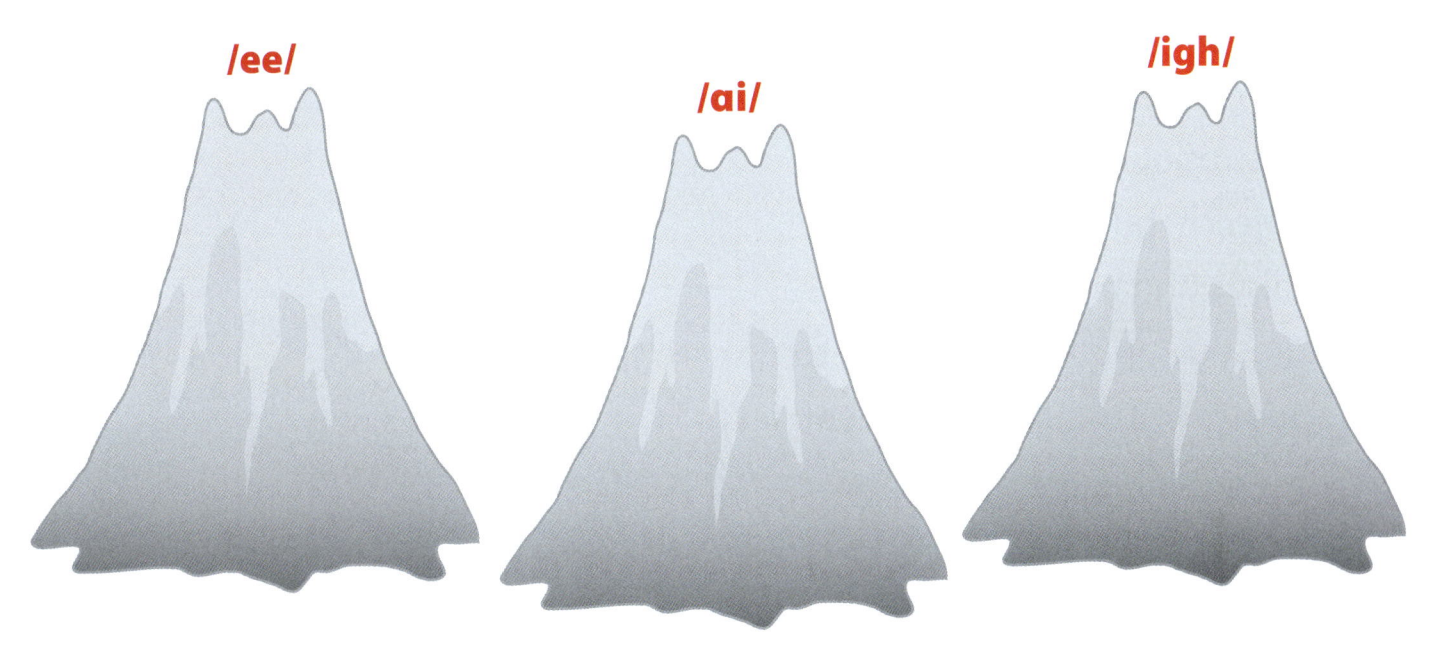

/ee/   /ai/   /igh/

C Explanation text is often written in the present tense. Rewrite the following sentences changing the verb into the present tense.

1 Dante II explored the volcano.

_____

2 The robot collected rock samples.

_____

3 The scientists remained in the control room.

_____

Non-fiction Reading

How to Create a 3D World

Jon Stuart lives and works in Brighton, in England. Jon creates amazing illustrations for the series *Project X*, but he doesn't use paints and paper. He uses the latest computer technology to create a virtual world that you feel you could almost walk into.

England
Brighton

Jon lives here!   Jon

Members of Team X.

1 First, Jon uses the computer to create a skeleton for one of the characters. The skeleton is then covered in skin and clothes. When Jon moves the skeleton, the skin and clothes move with it.

Because the character has a skeleton, it can move like a real person. Jon moves the skeleton into a pose to show the character sitting, pointing, looking startled, and so on. He can spin the character round to look at it from every angle and then choose the angle that suits the story.

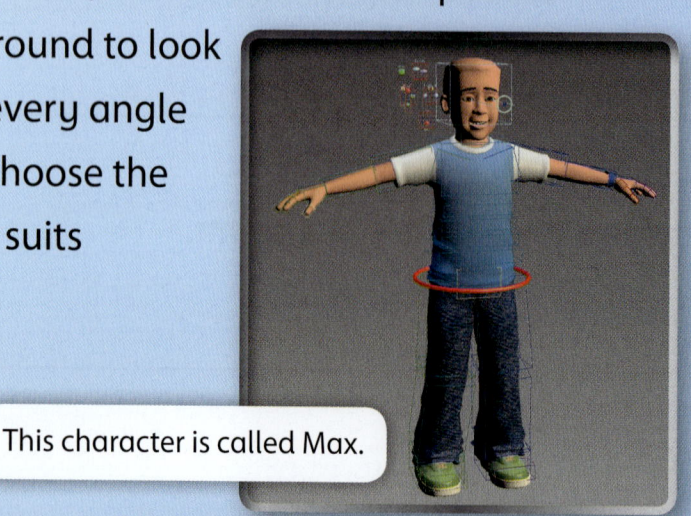

This character is called Max.

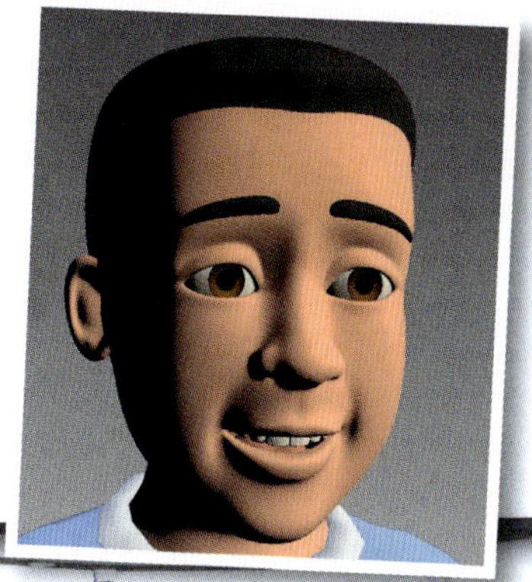

Non-fiction Reading

2 Jon zooms in on the face and creates Max's expression. He can move the jaw and eyebrows to create the look he wants – for example, cheeky, upset, happy or confused.

3 It's time to put the character into a setting. Jon has created each of the settings in the book. Each scene has been created like a virtual film set on the computer. Jon can move around the set and choose which angle he would like to see it from.

This setting is the inside of Team X's spaceship.

Like a movie set, each setting has different lights that can be turned up or down and angled. The lights can throw shadows and add atmosphere to the scene.

4 Jon places the characters, gadgets and robots in the setting and the scene is set. For a final touch, Jon moves the eyes of the characters to show where they are looking.

Non-fiction Reading

5 When Jon is happy with what he sees on the computer he asks the computer to select that scene and turn it into an illustration that will go into a school reading book. The books are in a series called *Project X*.

Max in a scene from the *Alien Adventures* books.

Max, Cat, Ant and Tiger in *Alien Adventures*.

Word Cloud

angle   scene
atmosphere   startled
expression   virtual world

Non-fiction Comprehension

How to Create a 3D World

A Read and respond

Number these actions to show the order in which Jon does them.

☐ Jon creates the character's expression.

☐ Jon puts skin and clothes on the skeleton.

☐ Jon creates the skeleton for the character.

B Read and respond

Find one phrase that makes the explanation sound interesting for the reader.

_____

C What do you think?

Re-read sections 1, 2 and 3 on pages 78–79. Write notes below to explain what each paragraph is about. The first one has been done for you.

1 *Creating a skeleton* _____

2 _____

3 _____

Non-fiction Vocabulary, speaking and listening

Word detective

A Tick each of these features of explanation texts when you find it in **How to Create a 3D World**.

Present tense ☐   Illustration ☐

Time words ☐   Technical words ☐

B Explanations often use technical words. Find these technical words in **How to Create a 3D World**. With a partner, look up the words in a dictionary and talk about what they mean.

illustrations
pose
skeleton
gadgets

To find a word in a dictionary, look at the first letter of the word. A dictionary lists words in alphabetical order.

Non-fiction Writing and punctuation

C Imagine you are going to interview Jon Stuart about his work.

What questions would you like to ask him?

What _____

When _____

How _____

Where _____

Who _____

Remember to use a question mark after each question.

Non-fiction Writing

Get writing

How a toast-making machine works
Part 1

Look again at the labels on the diagram of a volcano on page 71. Then use the following words to label this diagram of a toast-making machine.

chopper   toaster   butter   plate   conveyor belt

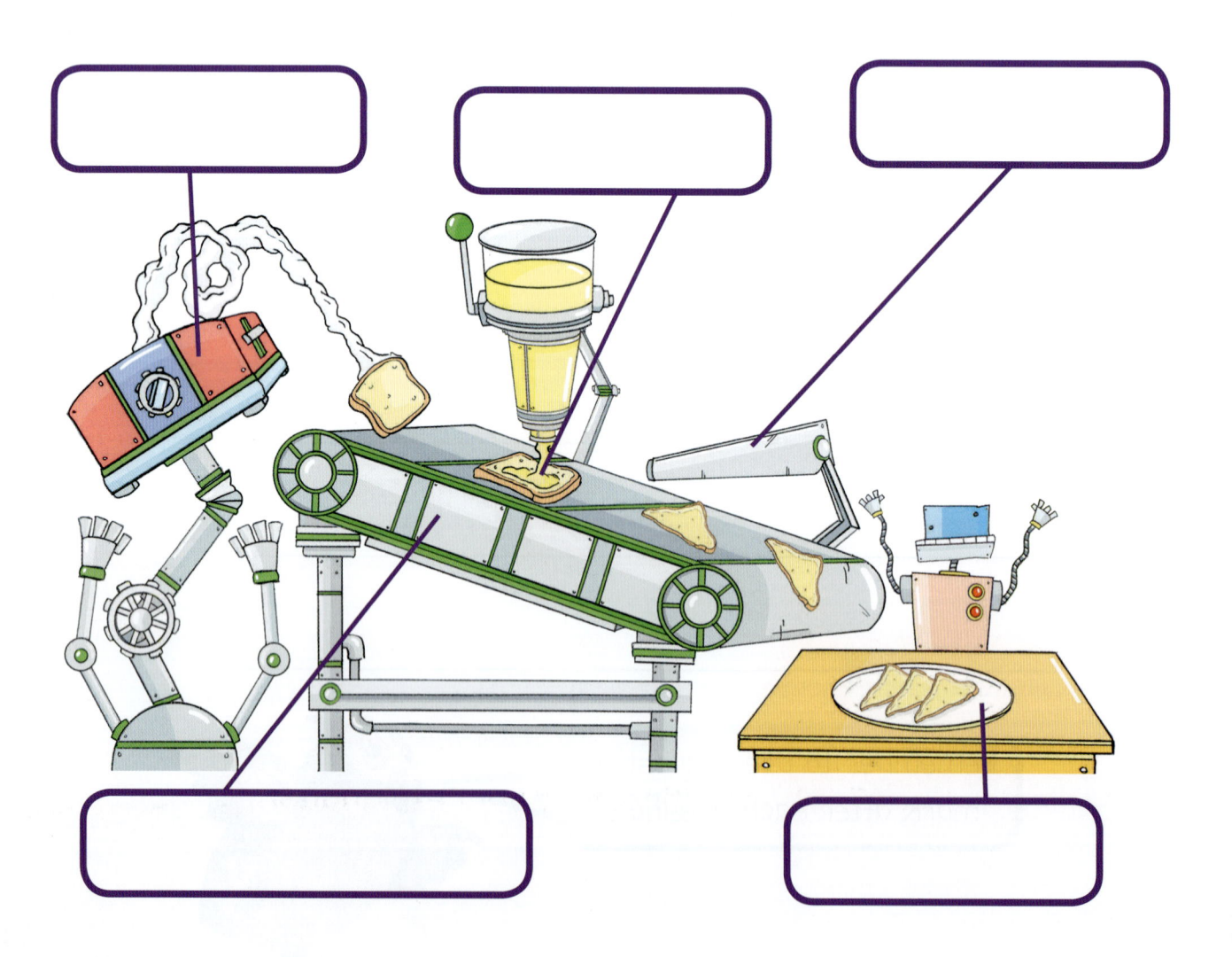

Non-fiction Writing

Part 2

How does the machine work? Write your explanation here.

First, the bread is toasted and pops out _____

Next, _____

Then, _____

Finally, _____

When you have finished writing, read your explanation to your partner. Does it make sense? Have you used present tense verbs and some technical words?

85

6 Caribbean trip

I'd Like to Squeeze

I'd like to squeeze this round world
into a new shape
I'd like to squeeze this round world
like a tube of toothpaste
I'd like to squeeze this round world
fair and square
I'd like to squeeze it and squeeze it
till everybody had an equal share

John Agard

Word Cloud
equal share

Flying Fish

Flying fish
flying fish
what is your wish?

In water
you swim
yet like to skim
through wind

Flying fish
flying fish
make up your mind

Are you a bird
inside a fish
or just a fish
dreaming of wings?

John Agard

Word Cloud
skim

Poetry Comprehension, speaking and listening

Read the poems **I'd Like to Squeeze** and **Flying Fish** on pages 86 and 87.

A Read and respond

1 In the poem 'I'd Like to Squeeze', which line is repeated?

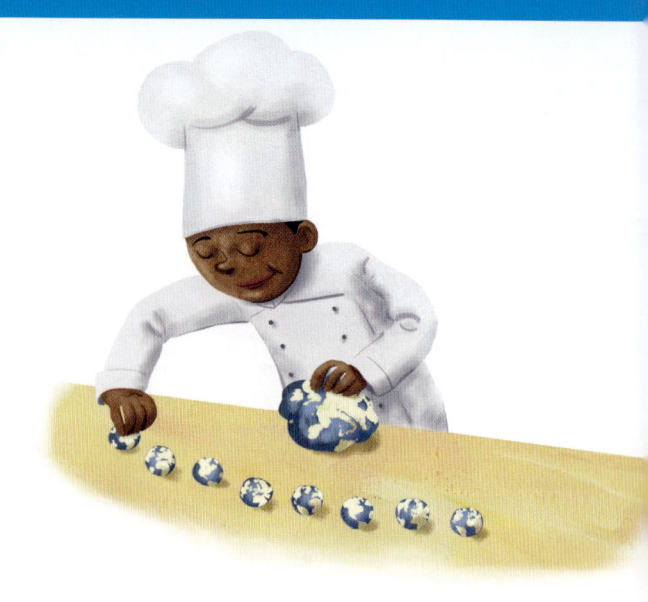

_____

2 In the poem 'Flying Fish', how does the fish move in the water?

_____

B Read and respond

1 In 'Flying Fish', why does the poet ask the fish if it is a bird inside a fish?

_____

2 In 'I'd Like to Squeeze', what does the poet want everybody in the world to have?

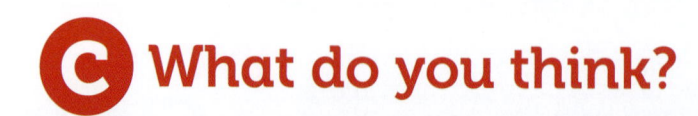

_____

C What do you think?

With a partner, discuss which of the two poems you like most. Explain to your partner why you like it.

Poetry Reading and vocabulary

Word detective

A Find one pair of rhyming words in each of the poems on pages 86 and 87.

_____   _____

_____   _____

B Underline the two words in each of the following lines that start with the same sound.

what is your wish?

like a tube of toothpaste

> Say the lines aloud and listen for the sound that is repeated.

C Show how the words below can be split up into syllables. The first one has been done for you.

fly)ing   toothpaste

everybody   equal

dreaming   water

89

Poetry Reading

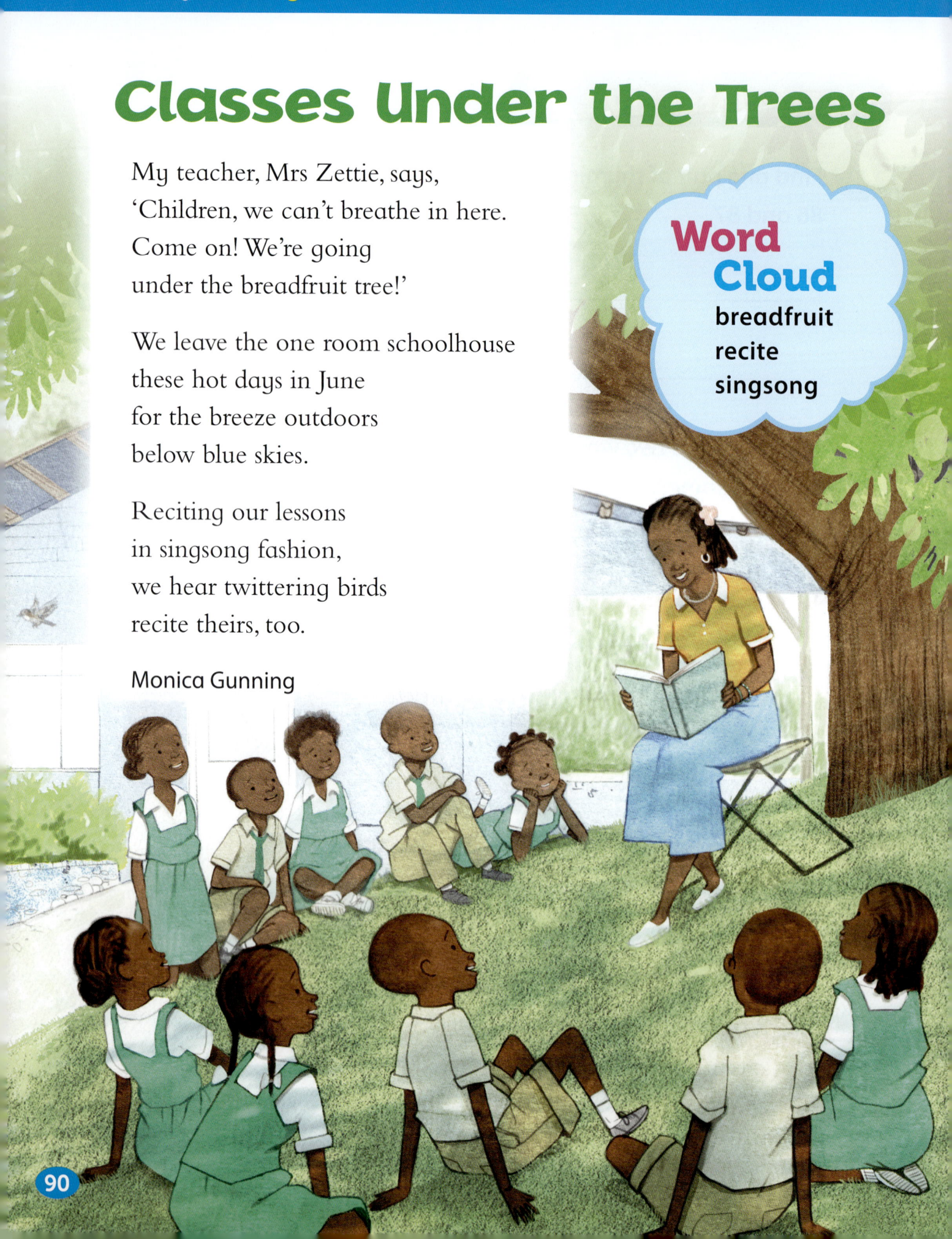

Classes Under the Trees

My teacher, Mrs Zettie, says,
'Children, we can't breathe in here.
Come on! We're going
under the breadfruit tree!'

We leave the one room schoolhouse
these hot days in June
for the breeze outdoors
below blue skies.

Reciting our lessons
in singsong fashion,
we hear twittering birds
recite theirs, too.

Monica Gunning

Word Cloud
breadfruit
recite
singsong

Poetry Reading

Water Everywhere

There's water on the ceiling,
   And water on the wall,
There's water in the bedroom,
   And water in the hall,
There's water on the landing,
   And water on the stair,
Whenever Daddy takes a bath
   There's water everywhere.

Valerie Bloom

Word Cloud

landing

Poetry Comprehension, speaking and listening

Read the poems **Classes Under the Trees** and **Water Everywhere** on pages 90 and 91.

A Read and respond

1. In the poem 'Classes Under the Trees', what can the children hear as they recite their lessons?

   _____

2. In the poem 'Water Everywhere', how many times is the phrase 'There's water' repeated?

   _____

B Read and respond

1. In 'Classes Under the Trees', why does the class go outside?

   _____

2. In the poem 'Water Everywhere', where is the water coming from?

   _____

C What do you think?

With your partner, discuss how you think the children feel about having their lessons outside in 'Classes Under the Trees'.

Poetry Vocabulary, speaking and listening

Word detective

A Find two interesting adjectives in the poem 'Classes Under the Trees'.

_____

_____

*Remember – an **adjective** describes a person, a place or a thing.*

B Find two compound words from each of the poems on pages 90 and 91. Write the two words that make up each of the four words.

1 _____ _____

2 _____ _____

3 _____ _____

4 _____ _____

C With a partner, take it in turns to read the poems aloud, clapping out the rhythm as you read. Which of the two poems you think has a stronger rhyming pattern and rhythm? Discuss your ideas with your partner.

Poetry Reading

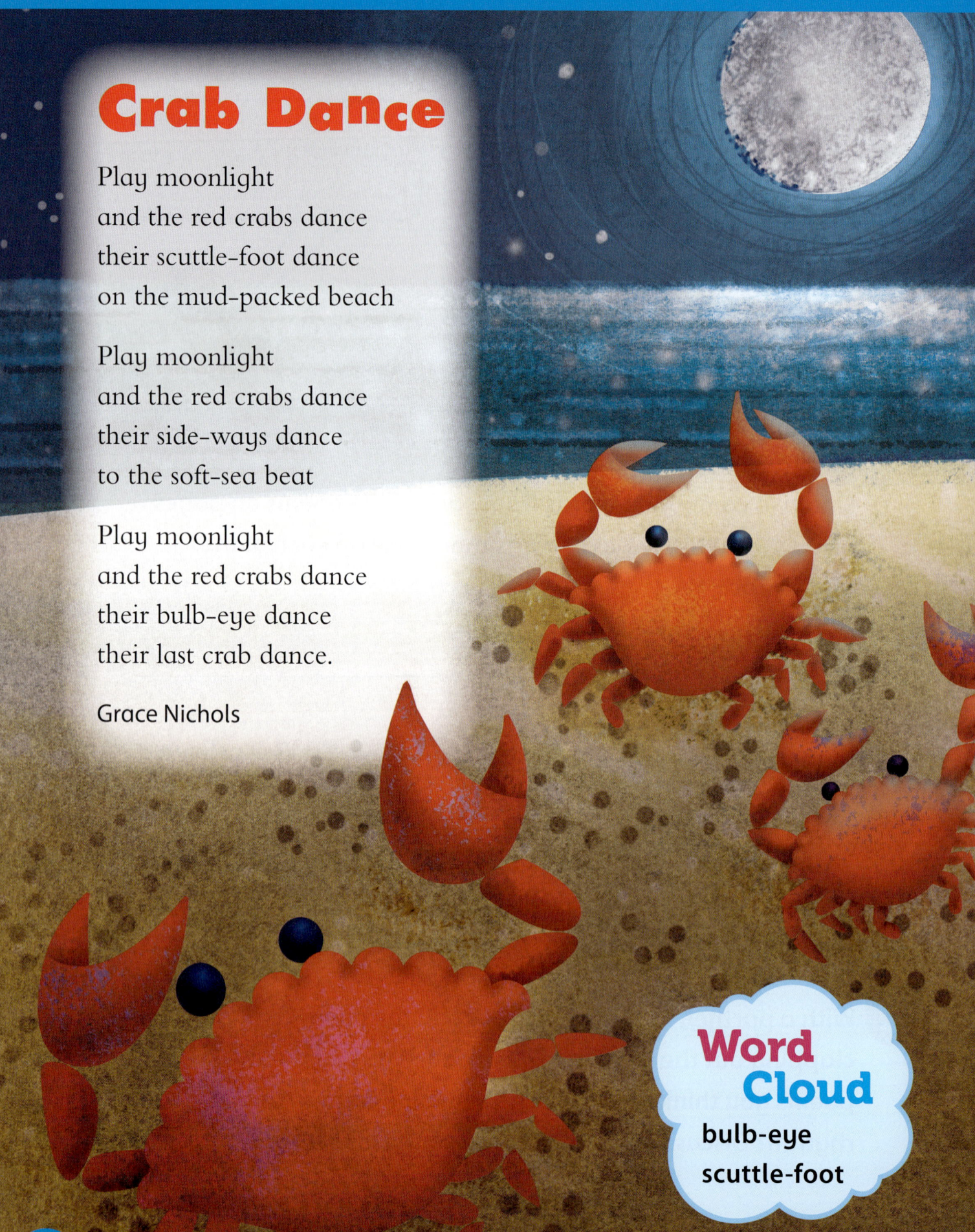

Crab Dance

Play moonlight
and the red crabs dance
their scuttle-foot dance
on the mud-packed beach

Play moonlight
and the red crabs dance
their side-ways dance
to the soft-sea beat

Play moonlight
and the red crabs dance
their bulb-eye dance
their last crab dance.

Grace Nichols

Word Cloud
bulb-eye
scuttle-foot

Granny Granny Please Comb My Hair

Granny Granny please comb my hair
you always take your time
you always take such care

You put me to sit on a cushion between your knees
you rub a little coconut oil
parting gentle as a breeze

Mummy Mummy
she's always in a hurry-hurry
rush
she pulls my hair
sometimes she tugs

But Granny
you have all the time
in the world and when you're finished
you always turn my head and say
"Now who's a nice girl?"

Grace Nichols

Word Cloud

breeze
parting
tugs

Poetry Comprehension, speaking and listening

Read the poems **Crab Dance** and **Granny Granny Please Comb My Hair** on pages 94 and 95.

A Read and respond

1. In the poem 'Crab Dance', where do the red crabs go to dance?

   _____

2. In the poem 'Granny Granny Please Comb My Hair', find two verbs that describe how Mummy combs the girl's hair.

   _____   _____

B Read and respond

1. With your partner, discuss what you think the phrase 'soft-sea beat' in 'Crab Dance' means.

2. In the poem 'Granny Granny Please Comb My Hair', how does the girl feel when Granny combs her hair? Discuss your ideas with your partner.

C What do you think?

With your partner, discuss which of the two poems you like most. Explain to your partner what you like most about it.

Poetry Writing

Get writing

Write a poem about fish swimming in the moonlight.
Use these words – or your own – to complete the verse.

silvery   sparkling

glistening   darting

Play moonlight

and the _____ _____ dance

their _____ dance

in the _____ sea.

Now write a second verse about children dancing on the beach.

Play sunlight

and the _____ _____ dance

their _____ dance

on the _____ sand.

97

Fiction Speaking and listening

7 Mountain bear adventure

Talk time
Do you think wild animals should be kept in zoos?

Fiction Speaking, listening and vocabulary

A With a partner, find the words on the left in a dictionary. Then draw lines to match the words to their meanings.

mountain	a place where wild animals are kept for people to see
adventure	a large, steep hill
zoo	an exciting experience

B

1 Write a word or phrase describing each of the animals on page 98.

Bear _____

Snake _____

2 Which other animals can be found in zoos? Write two or three here.

_____

_____

C Have you read any animal stories? Working with a partner, take it in turns to explain what happens in the story.

> Remember to ask questions and listen carefully as your partner tells you their story.

The Dancing Bear
Michael Morpurgo

Roxanne lived with her grandfather in a mountain village. One day, when she was seven years old, Roxanne found and adopted a wild bear cub. Her school teacher remembers the day it happened – it changed all their lives.

It was a Sunday morning in April. We were in the café before lunch. The old man was going on about Roxanne again, and how she ate him out of house and home …

"Gone off again, she has," he grumbled. "… Nothing but trouble, that girl."

Just then … Roxanne was staggering towards us, clutching a bear cub in her arms, with its arms wrapped around her neck. … She was laughing and breathless with joy.

"Bruno!" she said. "He's called Bruno. I was down by the stream. I was just throwing sticks and I felt something stroking my neck. I turned round and there he was. He patted my shoulder. He's my very own bear, Grandpa. He's all alone. He's hungry. I can keep him, can't I? Please?"

If we hadn't been there – and half the village was there by now – I think the old man might have grabbed the bear cub by the scruff of the neck and taken him right back where he came from.

"Look at him," he said. "He's half starved. He's going to die anyway. And besides, bears are for killing, not keeping. You know how many sheep we lose every year to bears? Dozens, I'm telling you, dozens."

Some people were beginning to agree with him. I looked at Roxanne and saw she was looking up at me. Her eyes were filled with tears.

"Maybe" … – I was talking directly to the old man now – "just suppose you made 'bear' labels for your honey jars – you could call it 'Bruno's Honey'. Everyone would hear about it. They'd come from miles around, have a little look at the bear and then buy your honey. You'd make a fortune, I'm sure of it."

I'd said the right thing. Roxanne's grandfather had his beehives all over the mountainside, and everyone knew that he couldn't sell even half the honey he collected. He nodded slowly as the sense of it dawned on him. "All right," he said. "We'll try it. Just for a while, mind." …

The cage was built in the village square and Bruno moved in. Roxanne looked after him as she had promised. …

Fiction Reading

Then someone wrote an article about Bruno in a local newspaper and there was a piece on the radio. People flocked to the village to see the bear, and the old man's honey sold out in a few weeks. …

Roxanne's grandfather was raking in the money.

Roxanne took no notice of any of this. So long as Bruno was happy, she was too. She lived for the moment after school each day when she would let him out of his cage and they would run together across the fields.

Often I saw them sitting together on a hillside. She'd be talking to him or singing to him, and when she sang now, she shamed even the skylarks to silence. Roxanne sang as I hope the angels sing.

Word Cloud
dozens
raking in the money
scruff of the neck
shamed
skylarks

Fiction Reading

Years went by and Roxanne and Bruno grew up. One day, a film crew came to the village to make a pop video for a pop star called Niki. The director wanted Bruno to dance for the video. Roxanne refused to make Bruno dance. The first days of filming didn't go well.

The Director blamed everyone: the cameraman, the sound man, the weather – even, at one point, Niki. By late afternoon he was talking of abandoning the whole project, packing up and going home.

… We all went home thoroughly fed up and dreading doing it all again the next day.

After supper, I was just going out for my evening stroll when I heard someone singing. It could only be Roxanne. No one sang like she did. She often sang to Bruno in the evenings before she said goodnight to him. The sound of her singing drew me down towards the village square. Roxanne was sitting in the cage with Bruno standing beside her, and she was singing Niki's song. I looked across the square. Niki was listening outside the café, the Director behind him. The entire film crew was there too. Roxanne saw none of them. As I watched, Bruno began to sway from side to side. Then Roxanne was on her feet and dancing too.

Fiction Reading

When it was over, Niki started to clap loudly, and then everyone did. ...

"That girl's magic!" exclaimed the Director as he hurried past me. "Pure magic." He liked that word.

"Did you see? He was dancing!" said Niki. "The bear, he was dancing!" Niki grasped the Director's arm and they stopped close by me. "I have an idea," he whispered. ...

"Her and you together," said the Director.

...

"Go on, you go and ask her; and don't take no for an answer. ...

I stood and watched from the shadows as Niki walked over to the cage. Roxanne was just closing the door behind her. She turned and saw him. "You startled me," she said.

"With a voice like that," said Niki, "you shouldn't be stuck away up here."

"What do you mean?"

He reached out and took her hands in his. "I want to ask you a favour," he said, his voice silky soft. "I want you to sing with me – you know, in the video."

"Me?" said Roxanne.

"When you sing," Niki went on, "everyone listens. When you sing the bear dances. I must have a dancing bear, and he only dances for you, doesn't he? I need you to sing with me, Roxanne. I need you."

Fiction Reading

"I don't know," she said shaking her head.

"It's easy," Niki went on. "You sing it like you did just now, but with me." He lifted her chin so that she could look him in the eyes. "You could be a star, Roxanne. You could be big, the biggest. Look what it's done for me. Everyone knows me. I've got houses all over the world: Paris, California, south of France. I've got four cars. I've got a plane. I can have anything I want. I can go anywhere I please. You could be the same. You could leave all this behind."

"No," she said turning away from him. "I can't leave Bruno; I won't."

Word Cloud

abandoning
blamed
grasped

Fiction Comprehension

The Dancing Bear

A Read and respond

Answer these questions.

1 Where is the story set?

_____

2 Who is telling the story?

_____

3 How does Roxanne's grandfather make money from the bear?

_____

4 What does Roxanne do after school each day with Bruno?

_____

_____

106

Fiction Comprehension

B Read and respond

Do you think Bruno is happy living in the cage? Write your ideas here.

_____

_____

_____

C What do you think?

How do you think the story will end? Will Roxanne go with Niki to become a pop star? What will happen to Bruno? Write your ideas here.

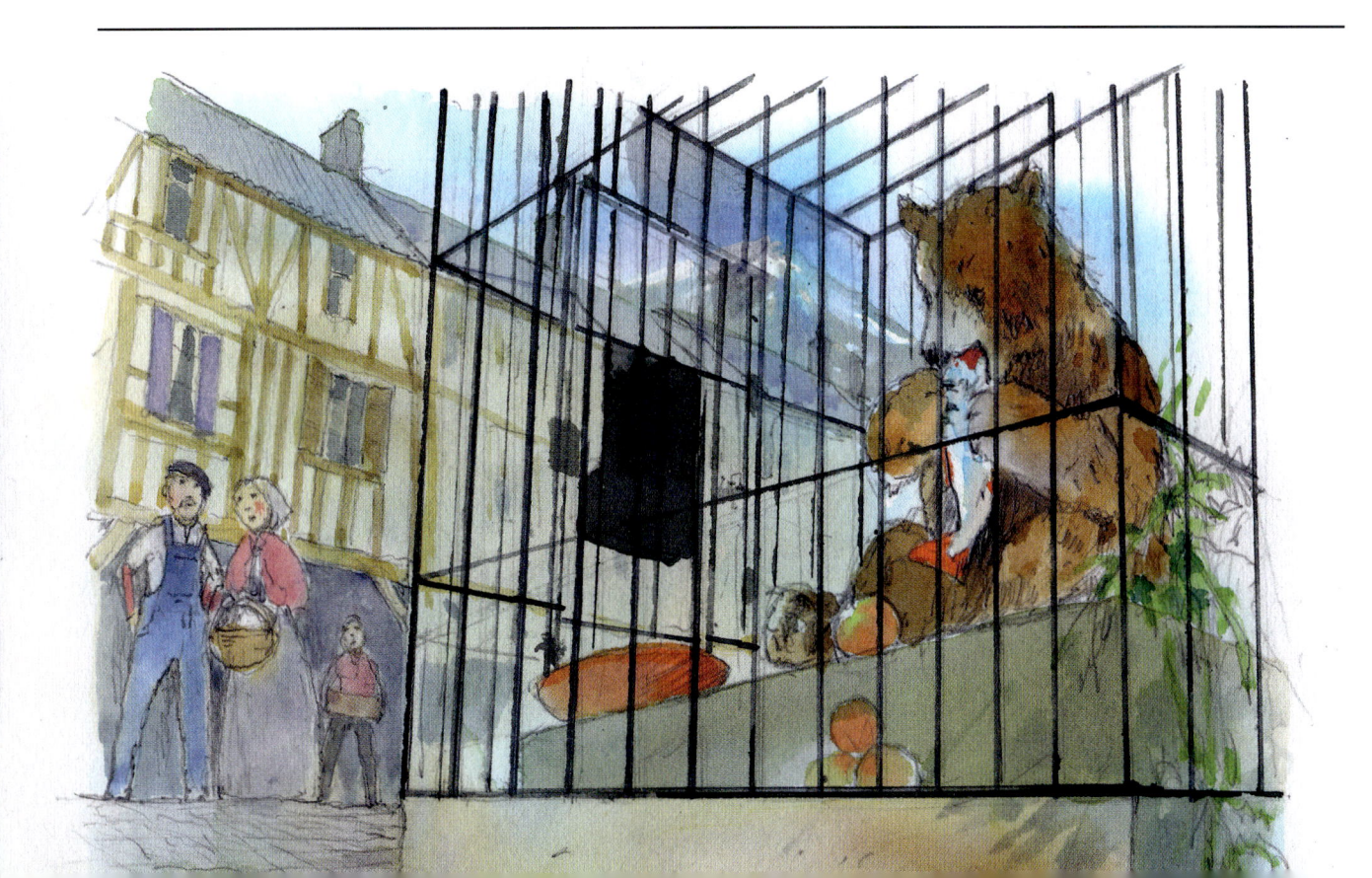

_____

_____

Fiction Vocabulary and spelling

Word detective

A

1 Words that have **–ful** at the end mean 'full of something'. Add the letters **–ful** to the following words.

> care   joy   beauty

_____   _____   _____

2 Words ending in **–ly** tell you how something is done. They are called **adverbs**. Turn these words into adverbs by adding **–ly**.

> glad   terrible   hungry

_____   _____   _____

> Remember these rules when adding **–ful** and **–ly**:
>
> When a word ends in 'y' change the 'y' to an 'i' before adding **–ful** or **–ly** (plentiful, easily).
>
> When adding **–ly**, if a word ends in 'le' (e.g. gentle), drop the 'e' and add 'y' (gently).

Fiction Vocabulary

B

1 Find two time words or phrases in the story.

_____

_____

2 Add a time word or adverb to the start of these sentences. You can choose from the words below or think of your own.

Time words and adverbs are often added to the start of sentences to make sentences more interesting.

| Kindly | Yesterday | Before dark | After school |
| Usually | Sometimes | Later | Cheerfully |

_____ Leo went to his grandmother's house for supper.

_____ she treated him to an ice cream.

_____ Leo walked home.

Fiction Vocabulary

C Write the following words and phrases next to the pictures of Roxanne or her grandfather. Add some interesting descriptions of your own.

> kind to Bruno grumbling
> pure magic interested in money
> fantastic singer mean

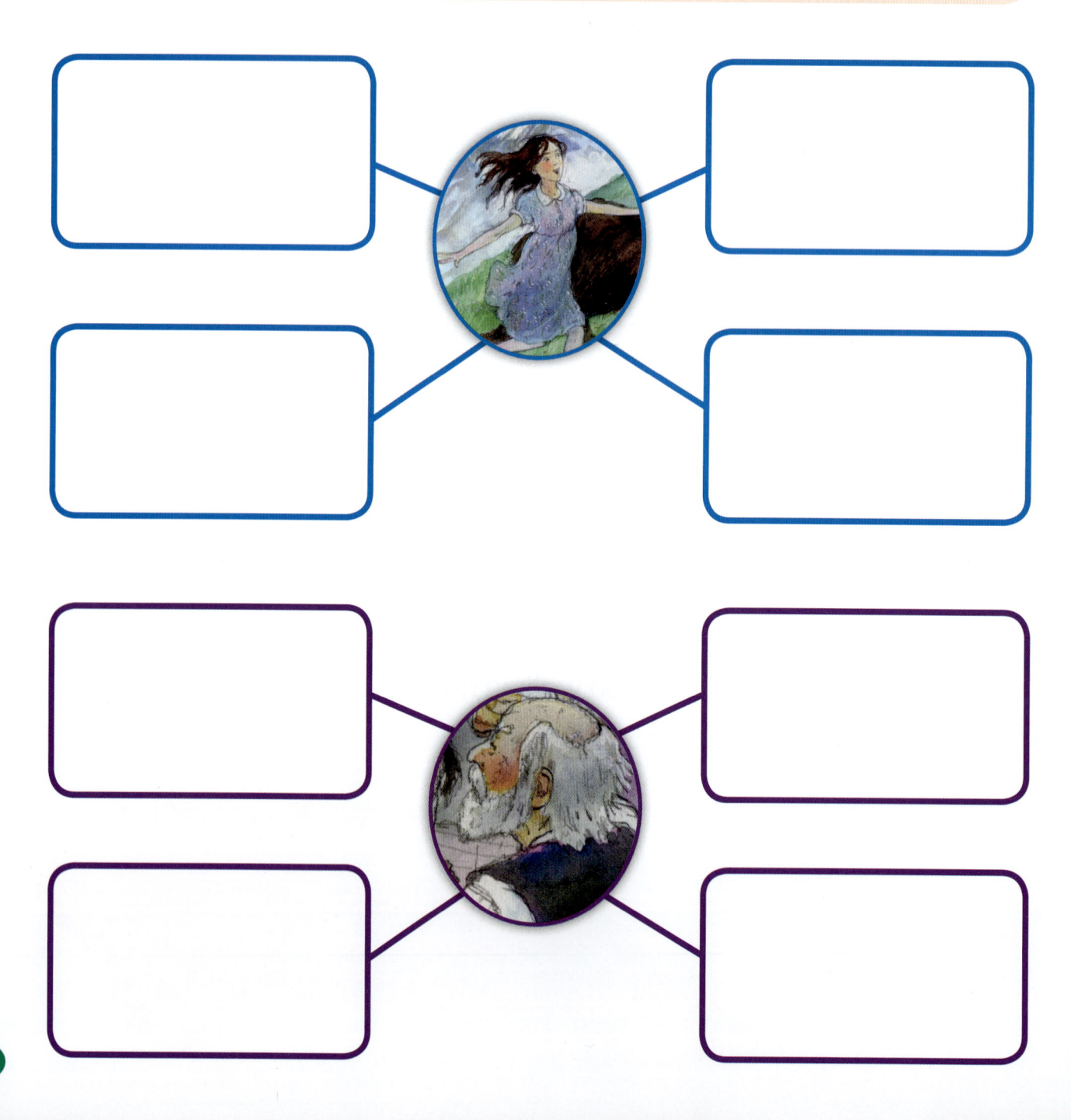

Fiction Writing

Get writing

Part 1

Think about a story in which a boy or a girl finds a wild animal and keeps it as a pet.

Where is your story set?

What is your character called?

What type of animal does your character find?

Where does he or she find the animal?

Where does he or she keep the animal?

What do his or her parents or carers say?

Fiction Writing

Part 2

Use the questions below to help you plan your story. Use a separate piece of paper if you need more space.

Beginning

Start your story off: say who your character is and where they find the animal. How does your character get the animal home? Include some words that will be spoken by your character.

Middle

What happens next? Describe where the character hides the animal. Include some words that your character's parents or carers say. Say what the character and animal do together.

Fiction Writing

End

How will your story end? Perhaps the animal scares away a bully or a robber. Will the character take the animal back to the place where it was found or to a zoo, or will they keep it?

When you have finished your plan, discuss it with a partner. Does it have a good beginning, middle and ending?

Now write your story on a separate piece of paper. When you have finished, read it aloud. Does it include some interesting words and phrases? Have you used some time words or adverbs at the beginning of sentences?

Non-fiction Speaking and listening

8 Animal world

Western lowland gorilla

Ivory-billed woodpecker

North Atlantic right whales

Talk time

If you could save only one of these animals from extinction, which one would it be? Explain why.

Non-fiction Vocabulary, speaking and listening

A Choose the correct animal name to complete each sentence.

> Ivory-billed woodpeckers   Western lowland gorillas
> North Atlantic right whales

1 _____ are very rare whales.

2 _____ have a long, pointed beak.

3 _____ live in rainforests in Africa.

B Look up the words on the left in a dictionary. Then draw lines to match each word to its meaning.

habitat	to look after
poach	the natural home of an animal or plant
protect	to hunt or catch animals illegally

C What is your favourite animal? Talk to a partner about why you like this animal. Discuss why animals are important to us.

> Remember to ask your partner questions and listen carefully to their opinions.

115

Non-fiction Reading

Animals in Danger

Many of the world's animals are under threat of extinction. Let's look at two animals that people are trying to save.

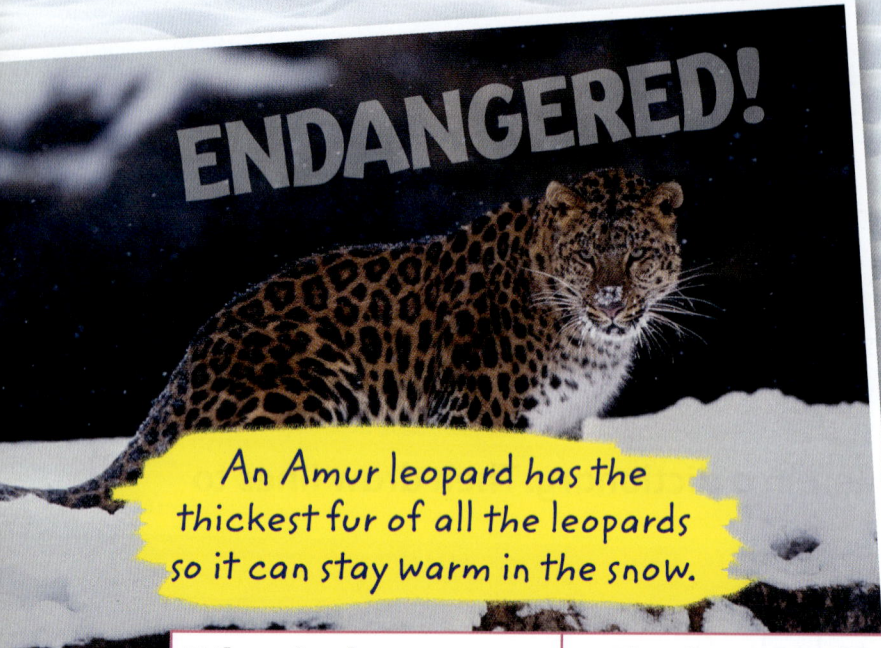

ENDANGERED!

An Amur leopard has the thickest fur of all the leopards so it can stay warm in the snow.

Amur leopard

Most leopards live in Africa but the Amur leopard lives in the snowy forests in Russia and China. They like to live alone and they travel a long way to find food. Their favourite food is wild boar.

What is the problem?	• The forests where they live are being cut down. • Hunters are killing them for their fur. • The food that they like to eat is becoming hard to find.
How many are left?	• About 65 animals
Where do they live?	• Russian Far East and China
How are they being helped?	• In one area 20,000 Korean pine trees have been planted. Wild boar love to eat pine nuts and Amur leopards like to eat wild boar. • In another area, a new national park has been created, called 'Land of the Leopard National Park'.

Non-fiction Reading

Javan rhino

Of the five species of rhino in the world, the Javan rhino is the most threatened. It lives in the tropical rainforests in Java and has one horn which is about 30 centimetres long.

What is the problem?	• Hunters kill the rhinos for sport. • Hunters kill the rhinos for their horns.
How many are left?	• About 50 animals
Where do they live?	• Java, Indonesia
How are they being helped?	• They live in a protected national park. Workers help to make this park as good as it can be for rhinos. • Some rhinos will be moved to a new park on a new island to create a new population of rhino there.

ENDANGERED!

The Javan rhino has skin that looks like armour.

Word Cloud

armour
endangered
extinction
national park
threatened
tropical
wild boar

Non-fiction Comprehension

Animals in Danger

A Read and respond

Draw a line to show where each bit of information appears.

Information	Where it is found
'Amur leopard' (words in red)	Caption
'The Javan rhino has skin that looks like armour.'	Chart
'Hunters kill the rhino for sport.'	Subheading

B Read and respond

Tick the sentence that is true for both the Amur leopard and the Javan rhino. Use the charts on pages 116 and 117 to help you.

☐ They are killed by hunters.　　☐ They live in snowy mountains.

C What do you think?

Using the information in the charts, think of a quiz question to ask your partner about the Amur leopard or the Javan rhino. Write your question below. Then take it in turns to ask your questions.

_____

_____

Non-fiction Grammar and vocabulary

Word detective

Reports about living things are written in the present tense.

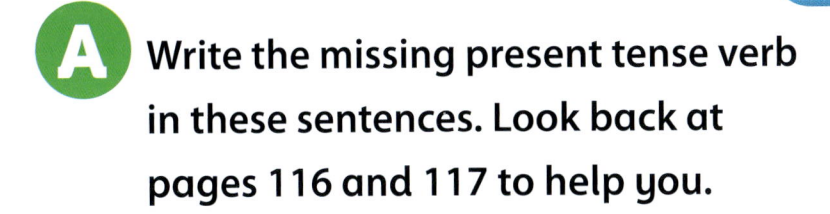

A Write the missing present tense verb in these sentences. Look back at pages 116 and 117 to help you.

1   The Amur leopard _____ in the snowy forests in Russia.

2   They _____ a long way to find food.

3   The Javan rhino _____ the most threatened species of rhino in the world.

B Show how each word below can be split up into syllables. The first one has been done for you.

thick)est   tropical

hunters   extinction

C Find a compound word in the **Animals in Danger** report text on pages 116–117 and then use it in a sentence of your own.

_____

_____

Non-fiction Reading

Red Pandas in Danger

Chilly home

Red pandas live in cold bamboo forests in the Himalayas, the highest mountains in the world. They mainly feed on the shoots and leaves of bamboo plants, but they sometimes eat birds and insects.

Hidden pandas

Red pandas can be hard to find because they are shy and secretive animals that mostly feed at night.

Threatened!

Conservationists believe there are only about 10,000 red pandas left in the wild. Over the last 20 years, half of the forests where they live have been chopped down. This means red pandas have less food to eat.

Red pandas spend most of the day asleep in trees.

What will the future bring?

Conservationists are asking the villagers who live near the red pandas not to cut down the forests. Other people are replanting new bamboo plants. Together they are trying to bring back a big area of bamboo forest.

Word Cloud
bamboo
conservationists

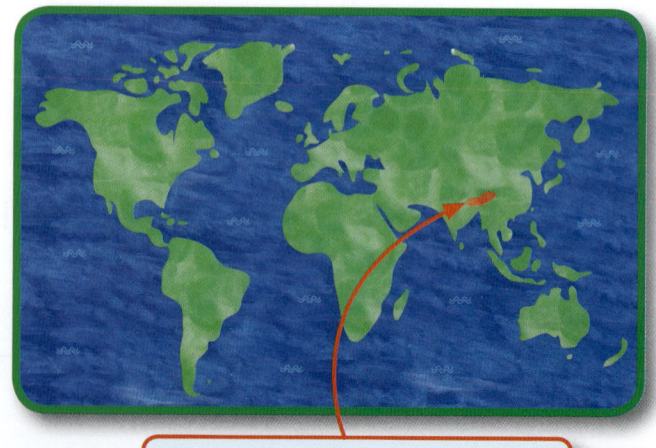

The Himalaya mountains – where red pandas live.

Non-fiction Comprehension

Red Pandas in Danger

A Read and respond

Circle all the non-fiction features you can find in **Red Pandas in Danger**.

- index
- map
- subheading
- caption
- photo
- chart

B Read and respond

Match the notes with the correct subheading.

Notes	Subheading
Live near highest mountains	What will the future bring?
Shy and hard to find	Chilly home
People replanting bamboo forests	Hidden pandas

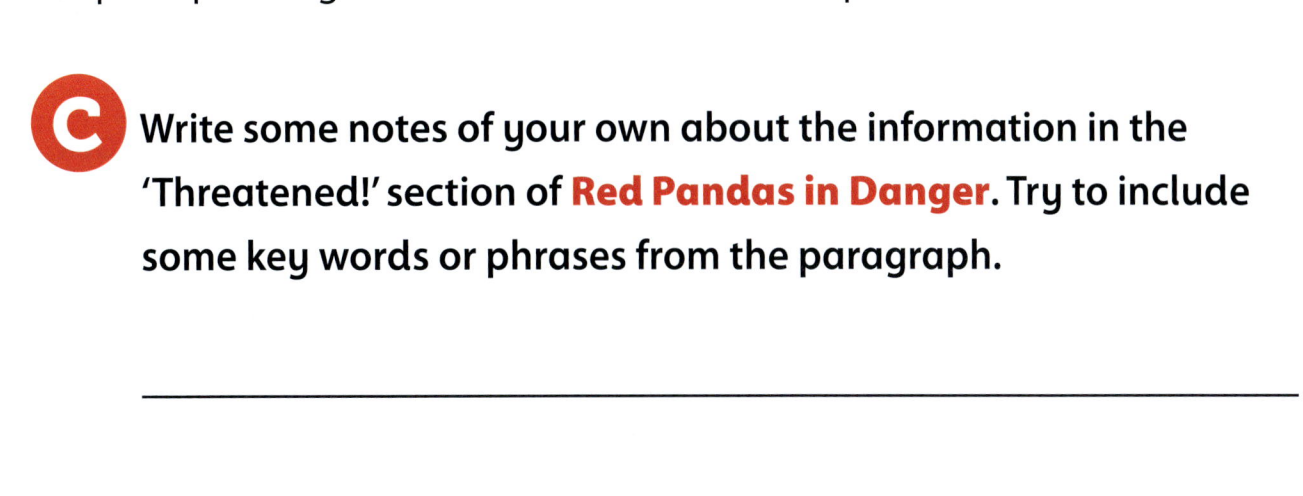

C Write some notes of your own about the information in the 'Threatened!' section of **Red Pandas in Danger**. Try to include some key words or phrases from the paragraph.

_____

_____

Non-fiction Reading

NGORONGORO CRATER

The Ngorongoro Crater, a huge grassy plain in Africa, is home to 25,000 animals. It was formed when an enormous volcano erupted over 2 million years ago. All that is left of the volcano is the rim around the outside.

Visiting the crater

Many people visit the Ngorongoro Crater to see the animals that live there. They stay in campsites or hotels called lodges.

The Ngorongoro Crater

The Ngorongoro crater is in Tanzania, Africa.

Word Cloud
campsites   plain
crater   rim
erupted

Tourists watch a black rhino in the crater.

Africa
Ngorongoro Crater
Tanzania

Non-fiction Reading

Animals in the crater

Most kinds of African animal can be found living in the crater.

Leopards live on the crater rim and in the Lerai Forest.

Ngorongoro Crater rim

Elephants
Hippos

Lake Magadi

Zebras
Hyenas

Monkeys
Baboons
Elephants

Lerai Forest

The crater is a safe place for the endangered black rhino.

Lions stay inside the crater because there is plenty of food.

Non-fiction Reading

Flamingos live on the lake close to the middle of the crater. Zebras stay close to other animals to keep safe.

Living in the crater

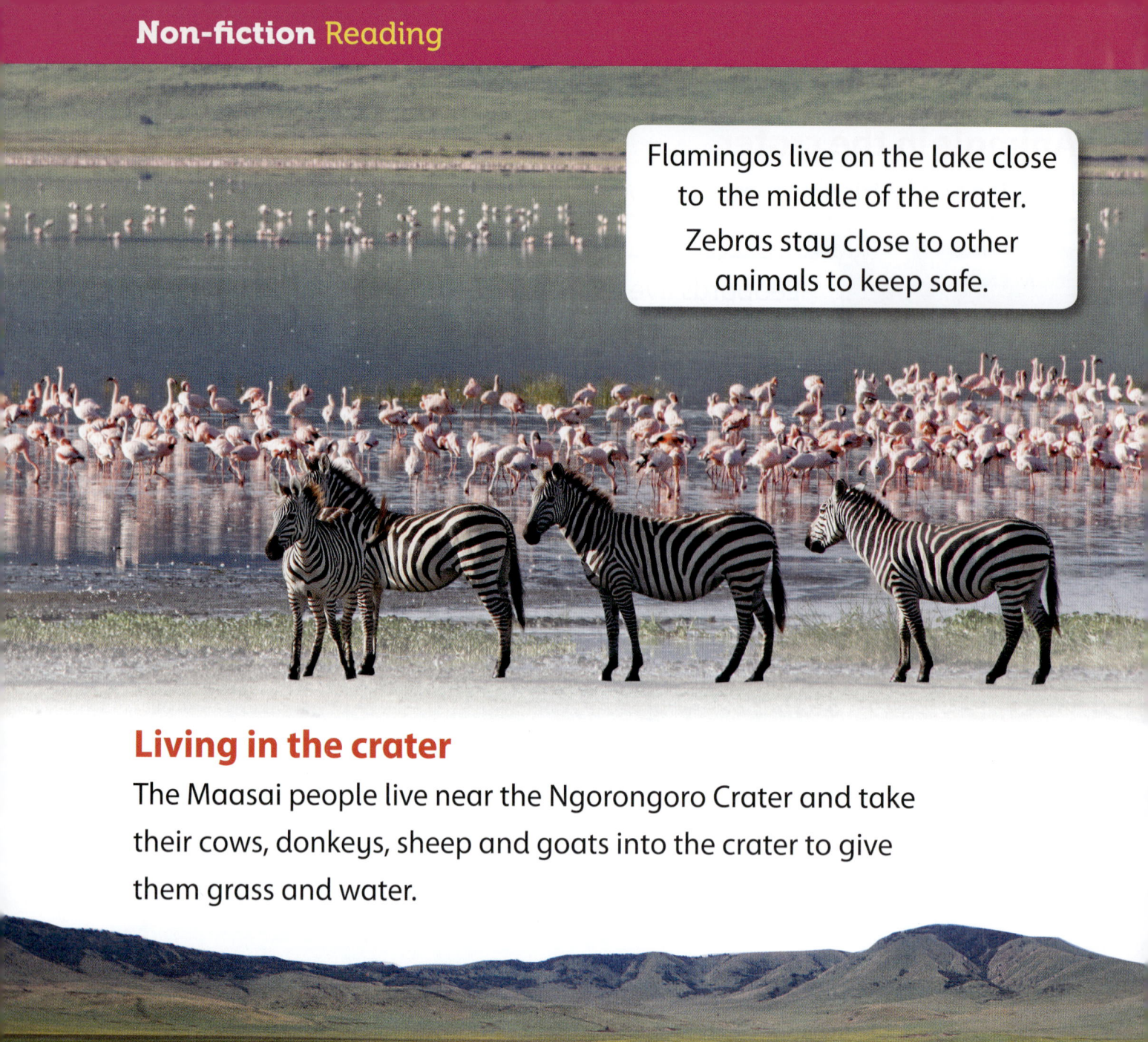

The Maasai people live near the Ngorongoro Crater and take their cows, donkeys, sheep and goats into the crater to give them grass and water.

Non-fiction Comprehension

Ngorongoro Crater

A Read and respond

Find the Lerai Forest on the map. Write the names of two animals you would find there.

_____   _____

B Read and respond

Which two sentences below are true?

		True	False
1	People visit the Ngorongoro Crater to see the animals that live there.	☐	☐
2	The crater is a dangerous place for the endangered black rhino.	☐	☐
3	Elephants and hippos can be found near Lake Magadi.	☐	☐

C What do you think?

1 What is the purpose of the Ngorongoro Crater text? Share your ideas with a partner.

2 Would you like to visit the Ngorongoro Crater? With a partner, explain why it is a special place and which animals you would like to see most.

Non-fiction Vocabulary

Word detective

A Replace the word 'and' in the following sentences with a better connective from the box below. Use each word once.

> **but   if   because   when**

1 Lions stay inside the crater [and] _____ there is plenty of food.

2 The black rhino is endangered [and] _____ the Ngorongoro Crater is a safe place for it to live.

3 Zebras feel safe [and] _____ they are close to other animals.

4 The tourists are happy [and] _____ they can see lots of animals.

Non-fiction Vocabulary

B Add *un–* or *dis-* to the beginning of the following words to make words with the opposite meaning.

> Letters added to the beginning of words are called 'prefixes'. The prefixes 'un–' and 'dis–' mean 'not'.

safe   appear   do   believe

_____   _____

_____   _____

C Replace the adjective in each sentence with an interesting one of your own.

1   The Ngorongoro Crater is [a huge] _____ grassy plain in Africa.

2   It was formed when [an enormous] _____ volcano erupted over 2 million years ago.

Non-fiction Writing

Get writing

Part 1

Write a suitable heading for the text below and add a caption next to the picture.

_____

The Cross River gorilla is the most endangered gorilla. The gorillas are hunted for their meat. There are only about 200–300 Cross River gorillas left living in the forests in Nigeria and Cameroon in Africa. These forests are being cut down. This means the gorillas get trapped in small sections of forest.

_____

_____

_____

Forest corridors are being created to link the small forests together. National parks protect the Cross River gorilla.

Non-fiction Writing

Part 2

Put the facts about the Cross River gorilla from **Part 1** into the chart.

Look at the charts on pages 116 and 117 to help you.

Cross River gorilla facts	
What is the problem?	•
How many are left?	•
Where do they live?	•
How are they being helped?	• •

Poetry Reading

9 Wordplay poems

Over My Toes

Over my toes
goes
the soft sea wash
see the sea wash
the soft sand slip
see the sea slip
the soft sand slide
see the sea slide
the soft sand slap
see the sea slap
the soft sand wash
over my toes.

Michael Rosen

Word Cloud
slap
slide
wash over

Poetry Comprehension

Over My Toes

A Read and respond

1. Which line is repeated in the poem?

   _____

2. What else, apart from the sea, washes over the poet's toes?

   _____

3. Which adjective is used to describe the sea and the sand?

   _____

B Read and respond

Imagine you are the child in the poem. What do you see, feel and hear?

_____

_____

C Read and respond

With a partner, take turns to read the poem aloud. Try to read with expression and listen to the sound and rhythm of the poem.

> Use your arms to show the sea washing over your toes and back again in every pair of lines.

131

Poetry Vocabulary and spelling

Word detective

A Find words in **Over My Toes** that start with **sl**.

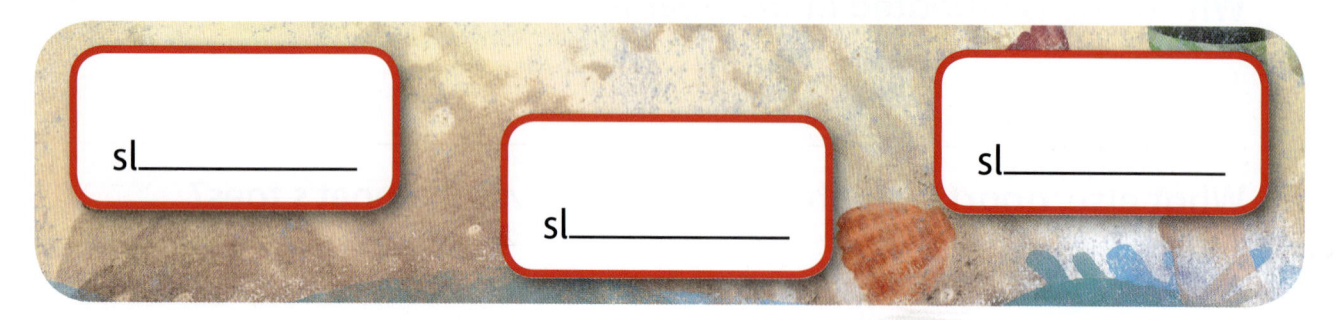

sl_____

sl_____

sl_____

B Circle the three words below that rhyme with 'goes'.

hose   glows   owls   nose   cows   growls

C Complete these sentences with **see** or **sea**.

1 We went out to _____ in our boat.

2 We could _____ Granny waiting for us.

Now write your own sentence using **see** or **sea**.

_____

_____

Tree Poem

the
leaves
have
all left
but
the
tree
will be
all
right

John Hegley

Name That Dragon

Dragons have the OLDEST names,
Dark as danger, fierce as flames.

Golden-fang or Spiny-tail,
Fury, Roary, Rattle-scale,

Sky-lord, Grabber, Princess-catcher,
Shadow-lady, Hero-snatcher,

Thunder-tooth or Smoky-jaw,
Smoulder, Scorch or Cinder-claw,

Leather-wing or Sorrow-maker,
Cavern-king or Treasure-taker,

Battle-queen or Mighty-biter,
Sword-snap, Bone-crunch, Fiery-fighter.

Dragon names are secret things,
Wild as weather, swift as stings.

Clare Bevan

Word Cloud

cinder   smoulder
scale   snatcher
smoky   sorrow

Poetry Comprehension

Tree Poem and Name That Dragon

A Read and respond

1 In the poem **Tree Poem**, what has happened to the leaves of the tree?

   _____

2 In **Name That Dragon**, which name describes a dragon's tail?

   _____

B Read and respond

1 **Tree Poem** is an example of a 'shape poem'. What shape do you think it has?

   _____

2 **Name That Dragon** is an example of a 'list poem'. What does the poem list?

   _____

C What do you think?

Which of the two poems do you like most? With a partner, discuss why you like it.

> Listen carefully to your partner's opinion and ask questions about their choice.

135

Poetry Vocabulary

Word detective

A In **Name That Dragon**, find the words that rhyme with these words.

catcher _____   stings _____

taker _____   jaw _____

B Find an adjective from **Name That Dragon** to describe these parts of the dragon.

_____ jaw

_____ fang

_____ wing

C Think of three words or phrases that you could use in a list poem about a tree.

_____

_____

_____

Night-lights

There is no need to light a night-light
On a light night like tonight;
For a night-light's light's a slight light
When the moonlight's white and bright.

Anon

Poetry Comprehension

Night-lights

A Read and respond

Tick the box to show if each sentence is true or false.

	True	False
It is a dark night.	☐	☐
The night-light makes a bright light.	☐	☐
The moon is bright and white.	☐	☐

B Read and respond

1. Which light does the poet think is brighter – the night-light or the moonlight?

   _____

2. Why isn't the night-light needed?

   _____

C Read and respond

With a partner, take it in turns to read the poem aloud. First read it slowly and then more quickly. Finally, read it together as fast as you can.

Poetry Vocabulary and spelling

Word detective

Remember, the long **/igh/** sound can be spelt in different ways: **igh** in high, **y** in cry, **ie** in pie, **i** in find, **i–e** in ice.

A Find the words in the poem that have the long /igh/ sound.

l_____   n_____

t_____   s_____

m_____   w_____

b_____

B Now add the correct letters to make other words with the /igh/ sound.

fl____   k____nd   cr____ ____d   pr____ z____

C Write a sentence using two words with the /igh/ sound.

_____

_____

139

Poetry Writing

Get writing

Part 1

Look back at the list poem on page 134. Then use these words to write your own list poem about a dragon. Combine one word from each list to create each name.

cave   fire   hero
cloud   treasure

fighter   hoarder   dweller
breather   toucher

_____   _____

_____   _____

_____   _____

_____   _____

_____   _____

Part 2

Now with your partner, think of something you would like to write a list poem about. It might be an animal, your favourite food, even your best friend!

> Your words don't have to be made up of two words like the dragon poem. It can be as simple as this:
> Brown
> Smooth
> Cool
> Sweet
> Chocolate icecream

Reading Fiction

Raju's Ride

Story by Pratima Mitchell

Pictures by Stephen Waterhouse

Raju and his baby sister were like the filling in a sandwich. Their parents took them to work with them every morning on a scooter.

When they got to their mango tree, Raju's mother and father got ready for the day's work and Raju went to school. The baby played on the blanket.

Raju went off to school with his bag on his back and a coin in his pocket. At break time he bought peanuts for himself and his friends.

Reading Fiction

All day long people brought their ironing to the mango tree. They brought sheets and shirts and saris. Raju's mother and father took turns to iron clothes all day long. The iron was very heavy. It made their backs very tired.

Parrots and squirrels and crows and doves loved the mango tree. They squawked and quarrelled. Sometimes they made a mess on the clothes. When Raju came back from school, he banged a drum to keep away the birds.

Reading Fiction

The children who lived in the big houses on the street didn't let Raju play with them.

"Go away!" "You're too young for our gang! Go and play with your baby sister!" they said.

Raju's mother said, "never mind them Raju. You'll get big soon enough. Let's take the ironing back to Mrs Sen at Number 30."

They left the baby with Raju's father and walked to Number 30.

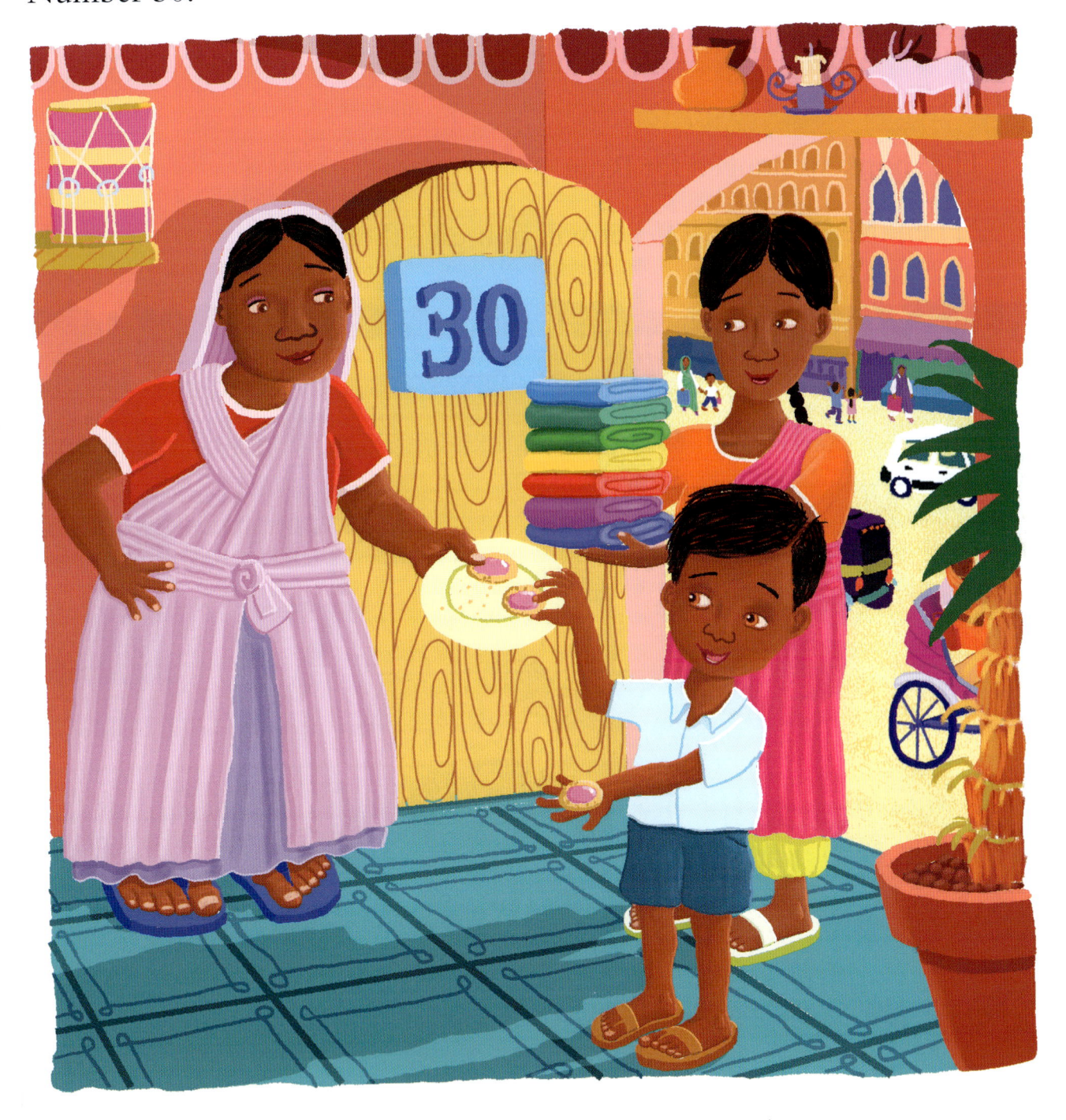

"Hello Raju," said Mrs Sen. "Done your homework? Here's a little treat for you."

She gave him three biscuits with pink icing on top. Raju smiled and said thank you.

Reading Fiction

When they got back to the mango tree, the monkey man was waiting in the shade.

"Look, Raju, look!" Here are the lovely princess and the handsome prince!" he said.

The monkeys danced for Raju.

"They need a reward! What will you give them?"

Reading Fiction

A cow came looking for something to eat. She saw the orange. But, before he could shoo her away, Raju's orange had gone into the cow's tummy.

The big children ran past rolling a hoop. Raju tried to run with them.

"No, you can't play with us. You're too young for our gang. Play with your baby sister!" they said.

Reading Fiction

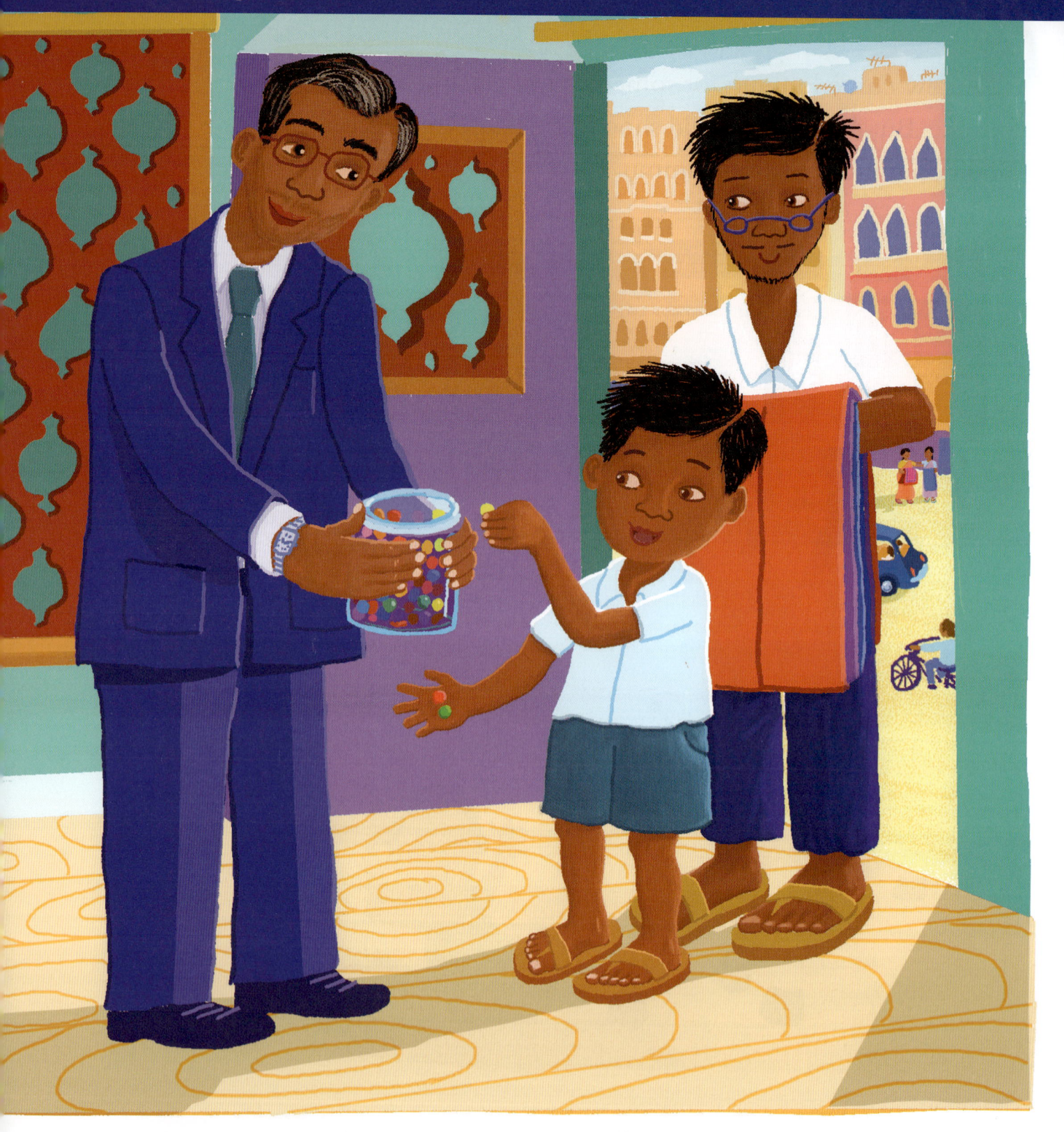

"Don't worry about them Raju," said his father. "Come, let's take these trousers back to Mr Nath."

Mr Nath gave Raju three sweets – red, yellow and green.

Reading Fiction

Raju left his sweets on the blanket next to the baby. All of a sudden, three fat doves flapped down from the mango tree. They each picked up a sweet and flew off. Raju threw sticks at the birds, but it was too late.

The big children were playing horses and carts. They galloped past Raju.

They cried, "You're too young for our gang! Play with your baby sister."

Reading Fiction

Raju's mother said, "Never mind Raju. Only one sheet left for Mrs Gupta. Let's take her back her ironing."

Mrs Gupta was having a tea party. She put a crisp, golden samosa in a paper bag for Raju.

On their way back to the mango tree, they stopped to say hello to Uncle Amir.

"What have you got there Raju?" asked Uncle Amir. "Yum-yum! I am so hungry."

Raju felt he had to give Uncle Amir a present. He gave him the crisp, golden samosa.

"Here's a present for you, Raju," Uncle Amir said, giving him a paper flag.

Reading Fiction

When they got back to the mango tree, Raju heard a very loud sound like a trumpet. Coming down the road was a huge grey elephant.

The elephant swayed from side to side. Its legs were like tree trunks. Its feet were like rocks. It was as high as the mango tree.

Reading Fiction

Reading Fiction

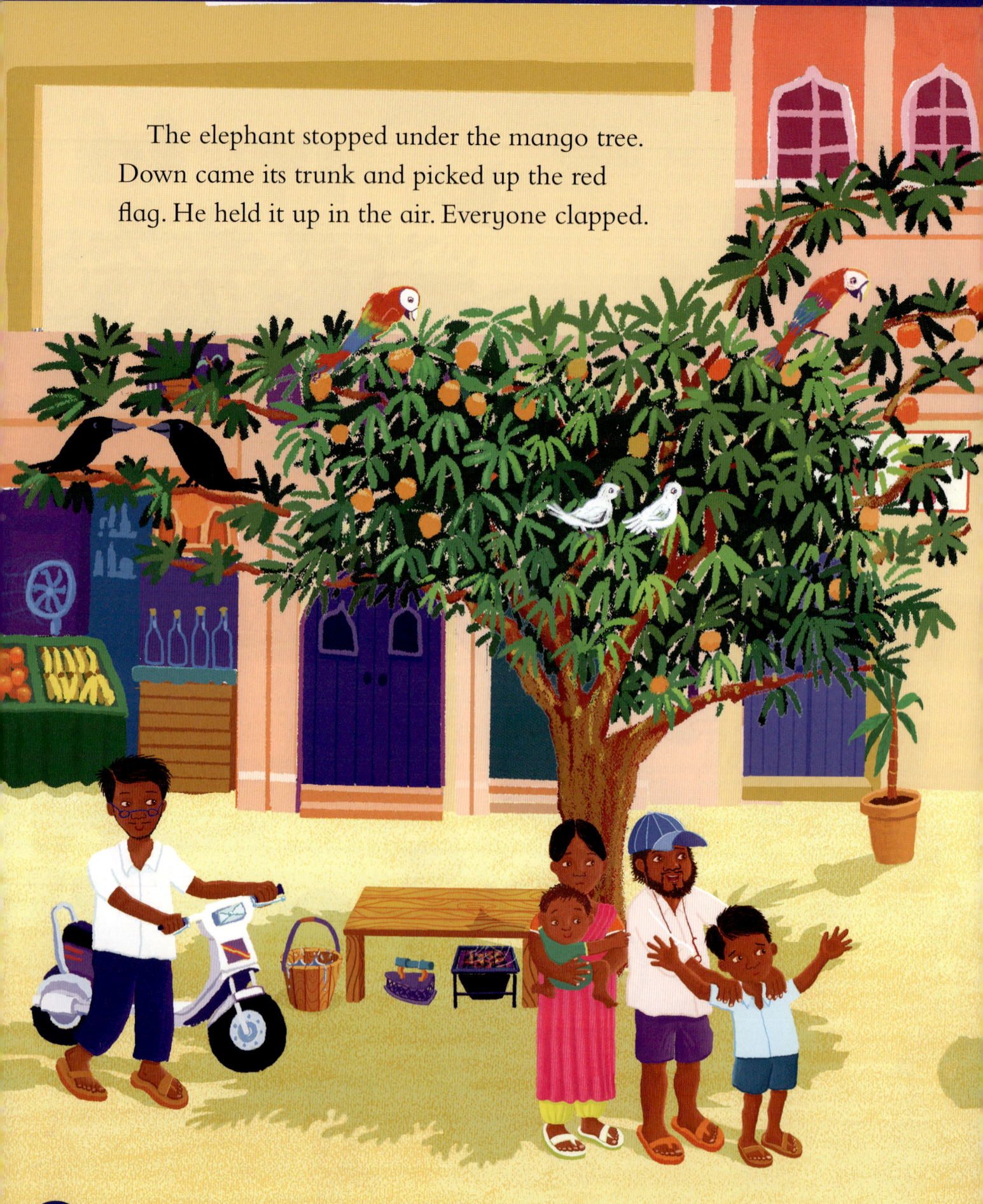

The elephant stopped under the mango tree. Down came its trunk and picked up the red flag. He held it up in the air. Everyone clapped.

Reading Fiction

"That's not fair!" shouted Raju. "First I had three pink biscuits. Then I had an orange. Then I had three sweets. Then I had a samosa and then I had a flag. Now I haven't got anything!"

He felt like crying.

157

Reading Fiction

Would you like a ride on my elephant?" asked the elephant keeper.

"You take Raju home on your elephant and we'll follow you on the scooter," said Raju's father.

Raju couldn't believe his luck.

The elephant kneeled on its front legs. The keeper helped Raju to climb up into the seat. Then the elephant raised himself slowly on all four legs.

The big children jumped up and down.

"Can we have a ride too?"

Reading Fiction

"No you're too big for my elephant," said the keeper. "This is Raju's special treat."

"Raju, Raju!" You're like a king!" cried the children.

They ran along beside the elephant.

Raju's mother and father and baby sister got on the scooter and followed behind. The bells on the elephant's neck jingled. Cars had to stop. Bikes had to get out of the way.

Reading Fiction

Raju waved at everyone. He touched the leaves on the trees. He felt like the most important person in the world.

Word Cloud

galloped   samosa
jingled   shoo
reward   squawked